ENDORSEMENTS

After enduring years of tough workouts with Jake, I was prepared for collegiate athletics. I was also able to handle any setback I faced, whether it was physical or mental.

Olivia Blackburn (Beyer)
NCAA Division 1 Volleyball Player at Louisiana State and Texas Christian University.
2019 Student Athlete of the Year
2021 All American

Jake is a continuous and life-long learner who innovates as a coach while staying focused on the importance of his core principles of always putting forth his best efforts, staying focused, and never quitting in the pursuit of worthy goals. Jake has valuable and unique experiences to share, and I know that many will benefit from reading about his journey.

David Hall
Managing Director at Alvarez and Marsal Disputes and Investigations.
Recipient of 7 Varsity Letters in 3 sports at The University for Michigan.
(Football, Basketball and Track)
Michigan Decathlon Record Holder
Quarterback of 1983 Rose Bowl
Daryl Royal Scholarship Recipient as an MBA student at University of Texas.

I first met Jake Sweeney at the Federal Law Enforcement Training Center (FLETC) in Glynco, GA, when I was head of the United States Immigration Officer Academy. He had earned the reputation as a strong (very strong) dedicated leader, superb physical techniques instructor and true professional. I did my best for the Immigration Officer Academy and stole him away from the Department of Treasury (who had recently hired him away from the US Border Patrol). One of the best "hires" I ever made!

Neville W. Cramer
INS Senior Special Agent & INS Deputy
Assistant Commissioner (retired)
and author of *Stop the Insanity*

Jake walked into my gym seeking only an opportunity. Within weeks, most clients would tell you it was his gym. I knew a lot. He implemented a lot. That's the Jake effect.

Terry Pratt, CSCS, CPT
Owner, Rejuvenation Fitness

Jake Sweeney bought one of my products years before anyone else. We felt we had invented something that was to change strength and conditioning forever. All of our early adopters were brilliant and courageous people because they could think outside the standards of an industry and have the brains to see why. This ability makes for the best leaders.

Jim Klopman
Inventor of the SlackBow and SlackBlock
Developer of the SlackBow Athletic Balance System
Author of *Balance is Power*

Jake Sweeney taught me the value of fundamentals as a youth hockey player. I still value those fundamentals today.

Matt Roy, Professional Athlete
Washington Capitals
National Hockey League

You're Allowed to Try

A Coach's Playbook on Discipline, Adversity, and Personal Excellence

Foreword by Lloyd Carr
Head Coach of the 1997 National Champion Michigan Wolverines

You're Allowed to Try

A Coach's Playbook on Discipline, Adversity, and Personal Excellence

Lawrence (Jake) Sweeney

You're Allowed To Try

Copyright © 2025 Lawrence Sweeney

Softcover ISBN: 978-1-950880-87-4
eBook ISBN: 978-1-950880-14-0

Scripture quotations taken from The Holy Bible, New International Version®, NIV®. Copyright © 1973, 1978, 1984, 2011 by Biblica, Inc. Used with permission of Zondervan. All rights reserved worldwide. www.zondervan.com

Scripture quotations taken from The ESV® Bible (The Holy Bible, English Standard Version®), © 2001 by Crossway, a publishing ministry of Good News Publishers. Used by permission. All rights reserved.

Scripture quotations taken from the (NASB®) New American Standard Bible®, Copyright © 1960, 1971, 1977, 1995, 2020 by The Lockman Foundation. Used by permission. All rights reserved. lockman.org

Scripture quotations marked MSG are taken from The Message, copyright © 1993, 2002, 2018 by Eugene H. Peterson. Used by permission of NavPress. All rights reserved. Represented by Tyndale House Publishers.

All rights reserved. No part of this publication may be reproduced, stored in a retrieval system, or transmitted in any form or by any means—electronic, mechanical, photocopying, recording, or otherwise—without the prior written permission of the author, except for brief quotations used in reviews, scholarly articles, or other noncommercial uses permitted by copyright law.

Printed in the United States of America

TABLE OF CONTENTS

Foreword. xi
Dedication xiii
Acknowledgements. xv
A Word to My Readers xvii
Why I Titled My Book xxi
Chapter 1. Discipline .1
Chapter 2. Make Others Feel Special 5
Chapter 3. Adversity 11
Chapter 4. Faith 21
Chapter 5. Fundamentals. 31
Chapter 6. Dream Big. 39
Chapter 7. Look Sharp and Look the Part 47
Chapter 8. The Value of Hard Work 61
Chapter 9. Commit to Finish. 67
Chapter 10. The Benefits of Being Coachable 75
Chapter 11. An Attitude of Gratitude. 83
Chapter 12. Power of the Posse 93
About the Author 101

FOREWORD

I've played for and coached with many exceptional coaches in my career. The great coaches are those who care about their players and challenge them to be their best. They push their players, encourage them, and lead them so that each one may reach his or her full potential. Jake Sweeney is one of those great coaches. He cares deeply for those that he coaches and personally invests significant time and effort into developing people physically and mentally to reach their performance goals.

I first met Jake in 1980 when he was a freshman at the University of Michigan. Jake was an offensive lineman and long-snapper for punts, field goals, and extra points. It was my first season coaching at Michigan. Our head coach was Bo Schembechler. Bo truly was one of the greatest leaders and football coaches of his time. Coach Bo trained his players hard, toughened them through repetition and drills, and made physical conditioning a cornerstone of the program. Bo also made all of us set goals, and then perform to reach those goals. Jake is a disciple of Bo's coaching philosophy. Bo didn't accept excuses; neither did Jake.

Jake possessed a unique skill honed through repetition and hard work: He was the best collegiate long snapper in the country. At that time, being a long-snapper was an afterthought for most teams and coaches. Not Coach Bo. And certainly not Jake. Being good, or even great, was not good enough for Jake. He desired perfection! Every day Jake worked tirelessly so that each snap was the same – same speed, rotation, and strings in the same place. For four years, every game, Jake never faltered. That discipline and work effort permeates every fiber in Jake's body.

As Jake mentions in his book, his grandfather and dad were coaches and teachers. They also were great athletes. Jake grew up in a family that understood the importance of hard work, toughness, training, and discipline. Some of the stories in this book touch on that grandfather-father-son/player-coach relationship. It's a special bond. Jake's handling of these relationships is one of the unique aspects of his book.

For Jake, he understands that greatness is more than just physical effort and training. The great athletes and people are those that also have mental toughness. Jake understands this and his mentorship and goal-setting skills discussed in his book have helped many people excel.

In closing, Jake provides lessons in leadership, mentoring, and goal-setting. The stories he tells speak to the fundamentals of success: hard work, perseverance, dedication, and a never give up attitude. He talks about working through adversity – something all of us face regularly. He challenges each of us to do the right thing and do it repeatedly. Thank you, Jake, for sharing your life lessons with so many people.

Sincerely,
Lloyd H. Carr,
Former Head Football Coach at the University of Michigan

DEDICATION

To my wife Dawn for allowing me the freedom to choose my own path, and always showing love for me and our family. I love you, always and forever.

ACKNOWLEDGMENTS

First and foremost, I would like to thank the Lord for always protecting me and my family (Psalm 91:4).

Next are my wife and children, who've endured hearing about this project for more years than it took me to complete it.

I would be remiss if I attempted to list all of my friends, clients, teammates, and the great men and women whom I've had the pleasure of serving with in the United States Border Patrol, Department of Treasury, and the United States Immigration Service.

Last, but not least, a special thanks to the "Big 5":

- Simon Presland, who helped me turn my ideas into outlined form that led to an actual written document.
- Darlene Deeg, for serving as proofreader while continuing to train with the adult class at the House of Iron.
- Paul Berry, who convinced me to take this project from the goal line to the endzone.

You're Allowed To Try

- Rich Hewlett, friend, teammate, and confidant for his constant words of encouragement.
- Finally, my publisher, Mike Owens and the team from AuthorSource Media. Thanks for helping me put this all together.

God Bless,
Jake Sweeney, May 2025

A WORD TO MY READERS

Teaching and coaching have been an integral part of my life. In fact, it could be said that those two professions are in my genes. Yet those were the last professions I aspired to. Those who knew my family assumed I would continue the family tradition and pursue these rewarding and challenging, yet often unappreciated, professions.

However, I was steadfast in proclaiming that there was no chance that I was going to pursue either of those careers. I told scores of people that I would never teach nor coach. Never. This is not the first time and probably not the last time that I will tell anyone who will listen: Never say never.

Now, I proudly embrace the fact that I am a third-generation coach. My grandfather, Lawrence (Doc) Sweeney, was an athlete, coach and teacher at Central Michigan University. He had such an impact on that school that a campus residence hall bears our family name. He was also credited with changing the name of Central Michigan University's mascot from the Bearcats to the Chippewas, in honor of the rich Native American heritage in the area.

My father, Mike Sweeney, was all-state in three sports at Mt. Pleasant High School and was inducted into the school's Athletic Hall of Fame in 1996. He made a career of coaching and teaching in Alma, Michigan. He coached football, basketball and tennis at Alma College and fared so well that he was inducted not once but twice into the school's Athletic Hall of Fame.

In the winter of 1976, my father motivated me to begin a training program that would bring me closer to my dream of becoming a professional athlete. He also provided a path that included setting goals, hard work, self-discipline and sacrifice, as well as incentives and rewards. It was a very simple and clear mission: Be willing to do the extra work, put forth your best effort, stay focused, never quit and your goals can be achieved. I thank God I learned this valuable lesson early in life.

    Unbeknownst to me at the time, my decision to accept and embrace my father's coaching would usher in a life that I have been blessed with, including the opportunity to have great coaches, mentors and leaders who have had a positive influence in my life. These people are as diverse in personality as they are in duty. Some are famous, some are unknown, some come from public education and athletics, some from business, while others come from vocations ranging from federal law enforcement to Christian leadership. I would be remiss if I failed to disclose there were times (too many to recall) that the coaching, advice and/or life lessons offered from these special people was not initially accepted or welcomed.

The purpose of this book is to share valuable lessons learned from and stories about these special people who have modeled the daily disciplines, strategies, leadership skills and lifestyles that have shaped not only my personal and professional life, but also those of countless others.

A Word to My Readers

I am forever grateful and fortunate to have known and learned from the people you will read about in the following pages, and it is my prayer that you find this work beneficial.

Lawrence "Jake" Sweeney
April 2025

WHY I TITLED MY BOOK:

YOU'RE ALLOWED TO TRY

Oftentimes we hear the statement, "You have to be willing to be uncomfortable, if you want to change." I most certainly have found this statement to hold true.

My first encounter with this "fact of life" was during a strength and conditioning workout as a freshman at the University of Michigan prior to the 1980 football season. Our strength and conditioning coach, Mike Gittleson, put us through the most physically and mentally challenging workouts I have ever been a part of. Near the end of these tortuous sessions, and when we were almost at the point of collapsing, Mike would inform us in a loud voice "You're allowed to try."

Certainly not the most profound statement, yet simple and to the point. When I first heard this, I didn't give it much thought; I was just trying to survive.

Over a period of time, I came to the realization that this statement was the starting point to turn a dream into a reality. The willingness to try something new and difficult is necessary for positive growth to occur.

Always remember, "You're Allowed to Try"!

Jake Sweeney
May 2025

CHAPTER 1
DISCIPLINE

"We are what we repeatedly do. Excellence, then is not an act, but a habit."

– Will Durant

Discipline: Orderly or prescribed conduct or pattern of behavior.

I'm a third-generation coach. My grandfather and my father made their livelihoods teaching and coaching at the high school and collegiate levels. Their success in these endeavors is evidenced by two important factors: First, their induction into athletic halls of fame as players and coaches. Second, and in my opinion the most important factor: The number of lives they positively impacted during their careers.

My college football coach, Bo Schembechler, often told his players that the measure of a successful coach was based on the types of fathers, husbands, friends and leaders his players became after their playing careers were finished. My grandfather and father also shared this belief.

A great coach or teacher has the ability to identify specific talents that a person demonstrates. A coach is then tasked to motivate players with the goal of enhancing their performance. A challenge for all coaches is instilling a disciplined environment to allow players and teams to improve their skills on a regular basis. I've found in my career that when athletes can recognize improvement over the course of time, after adhering to a regular practice or workout schedule, they are more likely to continue working to see even greater improvements.

I learned this firsthand before I began my high school career. My father, "Coach Sweeney," working at the college level at the time, recognized that I possessed athletic talent that needed to be developed if I wanted to be a star player in high school.

I started hanging around practices and games that my dad coached when I was six or seven years old. I always would tell whomever would listen that I was going to play football at Notre Dame or Michigan, then go onto the NFL.

I am certain my father heard me share these lofty goals and had already formulated a plan to help me achieve them.

He sat me down on the first day of summer vacation after the eighth grade and told me that if I wanted to be a great athlete, I needed to do extra work to get into better physical condition and become faster. He then offered me a deal: I could get into better shape and earn money at the same time. Needless to say, I was all ears.

He said that if I ran at least three miles, five days a week until football season started, he would give me $500 upon completion of this challenge. I only had to run five days out of seven days. I could pick my off days and all runs and off days would be recorded daily. I readily accepted this challenge and I'm proud to say that this ingrained a disciplined habit of strict adherence to a physical conditioning routine that I still practice today.

The first week of this challenge was extremely demanding, but as the summer progressed, I saw my physical stature, conditioning level and confidence soar. On the day the football season

Discipline

started I collected my $500 and showed up at my first high school practice a leaner, stronger and more confident player.

I accepted this challenge for four consecutive summers. In my final season of high school football, I was selected as an All-America and All-State offensive lineman and was awarded a full-ride athletic scholarship to play for the legendary Bo Schembechler at the University of Michigan.

I have fond memories from this period of my life and look back with a smile thinking about my father. Two things really stick out.

First, how doing something every day to get better can have a positive impact throughout your life.

Second, my father made an excellent return on investment by paying me $500 a summer to improve my conditioning. You see, the approximate cost of my four-year athletic scholarship at Michigan was $60,000—or nearly $250,000 in today's dollars.

Lloyd Carr, a great coach, leader, and friend.

What I've learned

1. We must be motivated to change.
2. We will invest time and effort if there is a reward.
3. Personal responsibility is mandatory while engaged in disciplined activities.
4. After we show improvement and see the benefits of hard work, we will become self-motivated.

What you can learn

- A new behavior practiced over time becomes a habit.
- Studies show that it takes 21 days to form a new habit and 60 days for that habit to become ingrained in the brain.
- When discipline becomes a habit, tasks become easier to perform with more powerful results.

Challenge question

What activity would you be willing to engage in, if you were certain that it would bring about positive change in your life?

Bible verse

Proverbs 13:1 – "A wise son heeds his father's instruction."

CHAPTER 2
MAKE OTHERS FEEL SPECIAL

"I have learned to imagine an invisible sign around each person's neck that says, 'Make me feel important.'"

– Mary Kay Ash

Can you recall an encounter recently in which someone made you feel special? As if you were the most important person in the room? As if this person was totally focused on you? And as if your time together was invaluable … to both of you?

I have been very fortunate to have met some incredibly successful people. These encounters are etched forever in my mind and share a common thread: The person I was meeting made me feel special, even though there were many people nearby, and those people were vying for his or her attention.

Making others feel special is an invaluable skill in developing relationships. Successful people from all walks of life must never underestimate this skill; it is a foundation in building strong, lasting and mutually beneficial relationships.

Several prominent leaders in my life come to mind, but one particular person made making others feel special the mission statement for a business started in the 1960s that's worth billions today. However, before I share "the rest of the story" of a memorable encounter with this person, I'll give you some background information.

I met Dawn Otten-Sweeney, my wife of 35 plus years (and counting), at the University of Michigan. However, our relationship didn't begin until we had graduated and entered the real world. Dawn had moved to Cleveland for a job in retail management. I was working at an automotive assembly plant in my hometown of Alma, Michigan, while awaiting the start of my first career in federal law enforcement.

We were engaged in the spring of 1986, just hours prior to my departure for Tucson, Arizona, where on May 19, I was to be sworn in as a Border Patrol Agent. After completing a six-month training stint at the U.S. Border Patrol Academy at Glynco, Georgia, I reported to my official duty station in Douglas, Arizona, a city located in southeastern Arizona on the Mexican border.

I find it more than ironic, unbeknownst to me, on the same date, May 19, 1986, my fiancé had chosen to start a new career by becoming a "beauty consultant" with Mary Kay Cosmetics. Suffice to say, our career choices were vastly different than those of so many of our fellow graduates of the business, technology and research-focused University of Michigan. However, I am happy to report that those decisions have positively impacted our lives, as well as many others, over the past three-plus decades.

Dawn and I worked very hard and advanced rapidly in our careers. After two years in Douglas, I was promoted to a supervisory training position at the Border Patrol Academy in Georgia. Dawn was promoted to the position of Sales Director with Mary Kay Cosmetics. During this time, she was awarded her first pink Cadillac from Mary Kay. 1

Early in Dawn's career, she had the pleasure of meeting and spending time with Mary Kay Ash, who founded her namesake company in 1963, at age 45, with a $5,000 investment. Dawn has always claimed that she has never met a more charismatic, kind and caring person. I eagerly awaited meeting this special woman.

That opportunity came at a dinner party on the Thames River in 1992. This was the first of more than 30 (and counting) reward trips that Dawn earned during her career as a Sales Director, Cadillac Sales Director and National Sales Director with Mary Kay Cosmetics.

During this evening in London, England, my wife escorted me to Ash's table. I was greeted with a radiant smile and she told me that she had been waiting to meet me for two years. I find it ironic that it was two years prior to this meeting that she "challenged" Dawn to become a top sales director so that she could bring her husband on the incredible trips all over the world that her company provided as perks to its leading performers.

After our introduction, Ash took my hands in hers and said, "I can tell that you're a special person. Always remember to love and support your wife, and she will make you a wealthy man."

She held my gaze with her bright blue eyes as I replied with a wink, "I am already a wealthy man."

She beamed her trademark smile and replied, "Yes, I can see that you are, and may God continue to bless you."

During that brief encounter, it became vividly clear to me how this woman from Hot Wells, Texas, had taken a dream at a time when women were an afterthought in the boardroom and built one of the largest cosmetic companies in the world.

You're Allowed To Try

I had the pleasure of spending more time with Mary Kay Ash during several award trips before her passing in November 2001. During each of these encounters, she would greet me by name, inquire about my family and my career, and most importantly, ask about my continued love and support for my wife. Her ability to connect with everyone she encountered and make them feel special was a gift she used to positively impact the lives of countless people during her long, successful and profitable lifetime.

Dawn and I with Mary Kay Ash in Bermuda, September 1994.

Make Others Feel Special

What I've learned

1. Everyone wants to be noticed, appreciated and respected.
2. When someone gives you their undivided attention, it shows that you are valued.
3. As a leader, it is your task to get results through teamwork. Making others feel important will help build mutually beneficial relationships.

What you can learn

- Listen with focused sincerity when interacting with others. No looking away, interrupting, waiting to respond or glancing at your phone!
- Show appreciation for the efforts, situations and concerns of others.
- Value other people's time by being prompt and prepared for meetings and appointments.

Challenge question

During the course of your daily interactions with others, do you attempt to make everyone you interact with feel special?

Bible verse

Matthew 7:12 – "In everything, therefore, treat people the same way you want them to treat you."

Postscript

1 My wife, Dawn, as of this writing, has driven a pink Cadillac, the signature vehicle of Mary Kay Cosmetics, for more than 35 years. Back in the day, Dawn started with a luxury sedan. Nowadays, she tools around in a loaded SUV. Our savings from this company perk in lease and insurance payments has exceeded $1 million!

CHAPTER 3
ADVERSITY

"There's nothing that cleanses your soul like getting the hell kicked out of you."

– Woody Hayes

Adversity: A state or instance of serious or continued difficulty or ill luck.

If you are alive on planet Earth, one thing is certain during your lifetime: adversity will find you and will become part of your existence.

Once we accept this "fact of life," we can learn to deal with this inconvenient and sometimes painful part of life and even learn to embrace it. When you learn to welcome adversity, you can use it to become a stronger person.

During coaching sessions with my clients, I make many correlations between dealing with adversity and physical training, such as:

- Adversity and physical training create stress on your body, both mentally and physically.

- The mind's response to continued mental stress is to become stronger and more resilient.
- The body's response to continued physical stress is to become stronger and more fit.

The major difference between physical exercise and adversity is that exercise is a choice you make that you control; adversity is an inevitable part of life that you have no control over.

If you want to grow through adversity, you must learn to embrace it as a tool to become mentally stronger.

Here is a short list of observations I've found to be helpful in dealing with adversity:

- Initially, it seemed insurmountable.
- I made a conscious choice to deal with it and its consequences.
- Dealing with it took less time and effort than I expected.
- I got through it … and learned from it.

The game of football taught me early on that adversity is an inevitable part of life that must be dealt with and overcome if you want to succeed.

As a high school football player, I was blessed with athletic ability, physical size, great coaches and a fair amount of luck. I traded my athletic prowess for a paid education at the University of Michigan, where I earned a starting position as a true freshman in the fall of 1980.

After the Wolverines' unexpectedly rough 1-2 start that season, our team ran off nine consecutive victories. These victories included a 9-3 triumph over the Ohio State Buckeyes

Adversity

in Columbus to win the Big Ten championship and earn a trip to the 1981 Rose Bowl in Pasadena, California.

Adversity met me head-on between the Ohio State victory and the 67th Rose Bowl on New Year's Day… and very well could have altered the trajectory of my life.

In retrospect, this painful event seems quite minor, and now I actually find it humorous. However, when this happened, it was very unsettling and I found no humor in it whatsoever.

During what we at Michigan referred to as bowl practices, I suffered an injury to my left knee. A teammate fell on my outstretched leg during a drill on December 19, 1980. When a football player sustains a knee injury, two thoughts immediately come to mind. "Oh my God, how could this happen to me?" and "Will I be able to play again?"

Most times, the mental anguish a player puts himself through after an injury is more traumatizing than the actual physical issue. Moments after this unfortunate situation occurred, I was helped off the field and into the training room to be examined by our team doctors and training staff.

This was the first time I had been injured in my athletic career. Needless to say, I was a basket case, laying in the training room, holding back tears and having a major pity party for myself.

Immediately following that day's practice, my pity party was crashed by none other than coach Bo Schembechler, who informed everyone within earshot in the training room, in a loud, agitated voice, "There is no way in hell that you're not playing in the Rose Bowl!" Then he bellowed, "Do you hear me, Sweeney?" He stormed out.

I was completely confused. I had no idea what to make of that exchange. Why was he so angry? Did he think I wanted this to happen? That I didn't want to play in the Rose Bowl?

Until this untimely event, I had never missed a football game or practice session due to injury. In fact, I had never even missed a quarter, let alone an entire game.

After a very long 48 hours and several painful tests on my knee, the doctors and trainers informed me that they felt I would be able to play in the Rose Bowl. Their diagnosis was a sprained medial collateral ligament, the one that provides stability to the inner knee. However, they also told me that I needed a full-leg cast to immobilize the knee to aid in healing.

The full cast was still on my left leg when our chartered flight left Christmas morning for Los Angeles. Before landing, I was told by the training staff to keep a "low profile" around our hotel and practice facility because I was on crutches. That low profile didn't last very long as a local newspaper reported that "freshman center Larry Sweeney arrived in California on crutches." Schembechler was quick to respond that the crutches were "only a precaution" and that I would be playing on New Year's Day.

I spent the first few daily practice sessions indoors with our strength and conditioning staff. Finally, with less than a week until kickoff against the University of Washington, the cast was removed. I looked in horror at my atrophied left leg which refused to bend. At this point, I was certain I wouldn't be playing on New Year's Day for the country's fifth-ranked team.

The next two days were filled with round-the-clock treatments (ice bags, whirlpools, electric stimulation) coupled with strength-training exercises. The pain was managed with anti-inflammatory medication and painkillers. I finally was cleared to practice and was taped up and sent out with the starting punt team, on which I was the long snapper. For those unfamiliar with this term, the long snapper sends the football between his legs, a distance of 14 yards to the punter.

I had barely walked since the injury, and our trainer told me to slowly jog down the field once I snapped the ball during practice for the punting unit.

Mere seconds after I snapped the ball to our punter, while watching my teammates sprint down the field, I fell flat on my face after being kicked in the ass by none other than Coach Schembechler. Not only did he kick my ass, but he also kicked me out of the remainder of practice.

This incident was the most humiliating moment I had endured in my 18 years of life. I was in shock while being driven off the field and back to the training room on a golf cart. My eyes filled with tears.

To add insult to injury, immediately after practice I was informed through an assistant coach that Schembechler had decided that I would not be accompanying the team to Disneyland, where the Michigan and Washington teams would be honored at a special function.

While my teammates boarded charter buses for an evening of celebration at Disneyland, I rode back to our hotel with a van of student managers and trainers. When I returned to my room, the tears I had been fighting back since being kicked in the ass and thrown out of practice flowed freely.

I had made up my mind: My time with the University of Michigan football program was over! I was getting the hell out! And getting out now before my teammates and coaches returned from the self-proclaimed "Happiest Place on Earth!"

My plan was really quite simple. I would call Grandma Sweeney and have her pay for a plane ticket back to Michigan. My grandmother was, until her death at age 96, the matriarch of the Sweeney family. After hearing my hysterical pleas for a ticket home, she agreed to get it with this caveat: that I would take one hour to think this through, be willing to accept the consequences of this choice, which included losing my scholarship to a prestigious university, and to say a few prayers to calm myself down. (My grandmother was a devout Catholic who attended daily mass for most of her adult life.)

After what seemed like a very short hour, I dialed the hotel phone to inform my grandmother that I would be leaving the team and heading back to Michigan. However, it was not my grandmother who answered my call, but my father, Coach Sweeney, and by the sound of his voice, he was not happy.

My dad did not even allow me to speak. He simply stated that if I were to "quit" I was not welcome back in Michigan—nor at his house. He told me that I should try to find a junior college team in California to further my athletic career. I tried to tell him how I had been disrespected and humiliated by Coach Schembechler, but I realized he had already hung up. I fell back on the hotel bed with my ever-present ice bag wrapped to my left knee and fell into a deep sleep.

When I woke up the next morning, my pity party was officially over. My attitude and demeanor had completely changed, and I decided that I would show Coach Sweeney and Coach Schembechler that their unsympathetic views toward my injury would not bother me, and I vowed to play the game of my life in the Rose Bowl.

On January 1, 1981, I played one of my best games of the season. We defeated Washington, 23-6, for our ninth straight victory and Schembechler's first in six Rose Bowl appearances. When I exited the locker room, I was met by none

Adversity

other than my dad, who gave me a congratulatory hug and told me how proud he was of me.

My father passed away on my 49th birthday. Not a day goes by that I do not think of him, the times we spent together and the positive traits he helped to instill in me.

He never once mentioned the phone conversation we had prior to the Rose Bowl.2

"Bo was intensity personified." The positive influence he had on me and countless other young men cannot be measured.

You're Allowed To Try

Bo Schembechler and I in the "The Big House" (Michigan Stadium) prior to the 1983 season.

What I've learned

1. Nothing worthwhile is accomplished until you learn to deal with adversity.
2. Adversity will force you to make a choice.
3. You ultimately are the product of the choices you make.

What you can learn

- Adversity is not pleasant; it makes you uncomfortable and it exposes your weaknesses.
- Dealing with adversity builds emotional strength and willpower; it forces you to deal with hardships.
- Adversity prepares you to accept new challenges ... and greater successes.

Challenge question

What consequences can you identify in your life that were the result of decisions made in the face of adversity?

Bible verse

John 16:33 – "In this world you will have trouble. But take heart! I have overcome the world."

Postscript

Just as my father never mentioned my frantic phone call from Pasadena, Bo Schembechler never mentioned the ass-kicking incident after the Rose Bowl during my final three seasons as a starter or over the decades before his death in 2006. As traumatic as the ass-kicking incident was at the time, I truly find it humorous these days. It makes for a great story, and not just in a discussion of overcoming adversity.

You're Allowed To Try

Coach Schembechler was intensity personified. His true genius came from his ability to motivate his players. He knew what buttons to push to get maximum performance from his Wolverines. When I was hurt on the practice field in Ann Arbor and didn't run down the field during practice in California, Schembechler determined that challenging my resolve was the best way to guarantee I would play in the Rose Bowl. He would make me so mad that I would do anything to prove him wrong. I hate to admit it now, but despite starting as a freshman, I, indeed, was kind of "soft." I hadn't dealt with any injuries, hadn't dealt with many disappointments, and hadn't dealt with this type of adversity.

To this day, I am forever grateful and take great pride in being one of "Bo's Boys", a name given to the chosen few who were mentored by this legendary coach and leader.

CHAPTER 4
FAITH

"No matter what has happened to you in the past or what is going on in your life right now, it has no power to keep you from having an amazingly good future if you will walk by faith in God."

– Joyce Meyer

Faith: Belief in and loyalty to God.

Any serious study of accomplished people would be remiss if it failed to include the role that faith plays in the lives of those who have achieved high levels of success. Some of these people are open and vocal about the role that faith plays in their lives. Others prefer to allow their actions to reveal the importance of their faith.

Having faith in something other than ourselves often comes through the trials and tribulations of life. In today's breakneck society, many of us tend to go it alone, attempting to navigate the inevitable storms on our own accord. Personal skills, work ethic, enthusiasm, charisma, physical might and intellectual gifts can help us achieve short-term success, but for long-term success, faith becomes a necessary element.

I like this quote and it's always relevant:

> "Sometimes painful things can teach us lessons that we didn't think we needed to know."
>
> – Amy Poehler

I laud and celebrate those of you who have found faith without enduring a painful life experience. I, however, was not one of these fortunate souls. As I often share with others who are navigating painful circumstances in their lives, sometimes we have to be brought to our knees in order to look up.

Here's my story.

In early 1986, two years after graduating from the University of Michigan, I realized my athletic prowess would not land me in the National Football League. I decided to pursue a career in federal law enforcement, and accepted a position as a U.S. Border Patrol Agent.

I was a lifelong thrill seeker, always looking for a new challenge. The Border Patrol was—and still is—considered the Marine Corps of federal law enforcement. Its six-month training academy is known for rigorous physical standards, Spanish language, firearms training and a law school-level immigration law program. The Border Patrol provided physical and mental challenges on a daily basis and I was once again a member of an elite team. The routine, discipline and camaraderie were exactly what I needed to help fill the void after my playing days.

In 1988, after serving as a "line agent" in Douglas, Arizona, I had the good fortune to be selected for a 12-month detail as a physical training instructor at the Border Patrol

Academy in Glynco, Georgia. When my wife and I departed the desert southwest for St. Simons Island, Georgia, little did we know that we would remain there for nearly a decade.

My new assignment: motivate and train newly hired Border Patrol Agents for the challenges they will face on the Mexican border. I was tasked with leading my "troops" through daily training sessions that included runs of up to five miles, calisthenics, interval training and the dreaded obstacle course. To make these tasks even more challenging, the training was performed in the oppressive heat and humidity of South Georgia.

As my year-long detail started winding down, I was offered a permanent position with the Department of Treasury at the Federal Law Enforcement Training Center (FLETC), the world's largest law-enforcement training center. After careful consideration and discussion with Dawn, I accepted this new assignment so we could remain in South Georgia, build a home and start a family.

In January 1991, Dawn and I celebrated the birth of our first child, Jake. At his first well-baby checkup, usually scheduled a couple of weeks after birth, his doctor told us that he heard a slight murmur while listening to Jake's heart. Assuring us this was normal and not of great concern, he still recommended seeing a pediatric cardiologist for a thorough examination.

We were scared, of course, but that was only the beginning.

During our appointment with the pediatric cardiologist, he told us that Jake had a congenital heart defect that, if left untreated, would be life-threatening. One or possibly two open-heart surgeries would be necessary to try to correct the defect. After the initial shock, Dawn and I vowed to find the best pediatric surgeon in the world. And as providence would have it, we were told that Dr. Edwin Bove at the University of Michigan's C.S. Mott Children's Hospital was the best of the best.

Dawn and three-month-old Jake flew to Ann Arbor, where Dr. Bove and his team determined that corrective open-heart surgery was necessary, but not until Jake was three months older.

With everyone back home, we tried to get back into our daily routines while anxiously awaiting Jake's surgery. However, the best laid plans often go awry. Less than two weeks later, Jake had a series of serious cardiac incidents in which he would have difficulty breathing, turn blue and lose consciousness.

Heeding our pediatrician's advice, we rushed Jake to the University of Florida Medical Center in Jacksonville. We then arranged transportation by air ambulance to Ann Arbor for emergency surgery.

After arriving in Ann Arbor, Jake was put in a pediatric intensive care unit, stabilized and placed "in line" for his emergency surgery. We saw babies with cardiac issues much more serious than Jake's and saw children die prior to or after surgery. Witnessing all this was gut wrenchingly sad and created a level of anxiety and stress that Dawn and I had never experienced.

After almost a week of waiting, the surgical team was ready to work its magic to fix our son's heart. Three hours later, Dr. Bove and his nurse emerged with great news: Jake's heart had been repaired and after a few days we could return to Georgia.

Back home, I immersed myself in my job with an unusually high level of intensity. In retrospect, I should have taken some time off and sought counseling to help me deal with the aftereffects of so many extremely stressful weeks. However, being an alpha male and a control freak, I chose to handle it myself, certain that, in time, my life would return to normal.

Sadly, over the next several weeks, I allowed my emotions to take control of my actions and my life began to spiral out of control. I was in dire need of a wake-up call … and it came in the form of a lunch date with Dawn. She shared in very clear terms that I was not the same man she had married and that if I chose to continue down the path I was on, she no longer wished to remain my wife. She advised me to seek professional help to deal with the anger, rebellion, disrespect and alcohol abuse that I exhibited on an almost daily basis.

Through tears of shame, I agreed to get help. Dawn recommended that I see Jim, a Christian counselor whom she had met at the church we recently started attending.

The pain that I was feeling, coupled with the shame that I felt from my recent behavior, helped me overcome the stigma I had attached to seeing a counselor. I've heard it said that "when the student is ready, the teacher will appear." I was ready to get my act together!

To say I was impressed with this man who helped me work through my issues would be an understatement. During our first appointment, I learned that Jim had served our country as a pilot in the Navy. He also said that God had called him to use his gifts and life experiences to serve others who struggled with the inevitable challenges of everyday life. After hearing this, I was motivated to meet with Jim on a regular basis.

Although I had never been around a man who shared his faith in God so openly, I admired his honesty and conviction. I also welcomed Jim's practice of beginning and ending each session with a prayer.

Unbeknownst to me, I was learning invaluable life lessons and insights from the teachings found in the Bible. Following Jim's direction, I began to read the Bible daily and apply what I learned relative to the tasks he assigned me.

I was a motivated student, and the issues that had plagued me in the past were slowly subsiding. One of the many beneficial takeaways from our sessions was a simple, yet effective, "priority hierarchy" list that I learned almost three decades ago and still use today.

Priority hierarchy:

1. God
2. Spouse
3. Children
4. Career
5. Service

Here is a brief summary for each of these priorities:

- God: Honor God in everything you do, that is your first and foremost responsibility.
- Spouse: Honor your husband or wife with love, respect and the gift of time.
- Children: Embrace your duties and responsibilities as a parent to love, nurture and care for your children while always attempting to serve as a positive adult role model.
- Career: Labor diligently in the position you hold to honor, respect and submit to those in authority.
- Service: Provide assistance to someone or something with an "attitude of gratitude."

The implementation of this simple, yet highly effective list, has helped me navigate the tumultuous world in which we live and become a better husband, father, friend and leader.

During my sessions with Jim, I came to realize that the majority of my issues stemmed from my attempts to control virtually all aspects of my life. Accepting that most things were not in my power to control was a hard lesson. However, as I continued to study the Bible, I further learned that human beings have only a few things that we can control completely.

To remind myself, I made a sign to display in the physical training facility that I own and operate. It reads:

5 Things You CONTROL
1. Your attitude
2. Your effort
3. Your actions
4. Your emotions
5. Your words

Seeing this on a daily basis reminds me of what I can control … and what I can't.

The growth pains during an extremely challenging period motivated me to confess my sins and ask Jesus Christ to be the Lord of my life. This is one of the best decisions, if not the best, of my life.

I'll be the first to admit that my life has been far from perfect since that decision. However, there is no doubt that I have become a better person, husband, father, friend and leader after submitting my life to Christ. I am forever grateful to my wife for possessing the courage and conviction and her gift of clear, concise communication in motivating me to seek the counsel of a focused, gifted and committed Christian counselor. Their actions together served as a catalyst that allowed me to choose a life I never imagined could be so rewarding.

Dawn and I at the ruins of the ancient church of Ephesus in Turkey.

Faith

What I've learned

1. Being a "control freak" is not an admirable personality trait and can cause problems in your life.
2. Pain is a great motivator.
3. A person is the product of the choices he or she makes.

What you can learn

Among the numerous benefits of being a Christian:

- Greater peace and joy in your life.
- Not being concerned with pleasing others.
- Enjoying more meaningful relationships with others.

Challenge question

Reflect upon a couple of major decisions you have made. What circumstances led you to make these decisions?

Bible verse

Hebrews 11: 1 – "Now faith is confidence in what we hope for and assurance about what we do not see."

CHAPTER 5
FUNDAMENTALS

"Get the fundamentals down and the level of everything you do will rise."

– Michael Jordan

Fundamentals: The basis of essential structure or function.

Reading is a lifelong passion of mine. I'm forever grateful for being exposed to reading at an early age. I spent many weekends with my grandmother, who was a teacher and a voracious reader. She had an in-home library filled with books of all types. Before I could read, she read to me for hours. When I could read on my own, Grandma had me read aloud to her. When I came across words I didn't know, she taught me to use a dictionary and a thesaurus.

The time spent learning to read fueled my passion for the written and spoken word, and it was no surprise that I always gravitated toward classes in school that focused on reading and writing.

As I think back, I was also fortunate to have had great teachers who mentored and challenged me from elementary school through college. Being the son and grandson of public-school teachers, I am forever grateful for the efforts of these passionate men and women who serve as teachers.

However, one teacher stands out among all others because of a valuable life lesson she taught me during my senior year of high school in 1980.

Mrs. Joan Snellenberger had the ability to motivate a diverse group of 17- and 18-year-olds to actually enjoy and look forward to senior English, where she challenged us daily to enhance our reading, writing and public speaking skills. Mrs. Snellenberger embodied "old school," the term I use to describe a disciplined, focused and tough individual who gives great effort and demands great effort from her charges.

During the course of the year, we studied Shakespeare's "Macbeth" and were required to read aloud the various characters from this great 17th-century play. Another literary classic we studied was "Long Day's Journey into Night," Eugene O'Neill's 1956 play, which raised our awareness of drug and alcohol addiction in our society. Mrs. Shellenberger required us to give an in-depth, oral presentation, a skill that still benefits me today.

We also had the dubious pleasure of completing a college-level term paper prior to graduation. Years later, I realized that Senior English was on par with the literature and composition classes I took at the University of Michigan. As a high school senior, the first couple of months of my second semester were especially exciting and hectic, as I was being recruited by several elite Division 1 football programs. Daily phone calls and visits from college coaches, coupled with six consecutive weekend recruiting trips, assured me that my goal of becoming a scholarship college football player was close at hand. Senior English immediately followed lunch and coincided with the time that most college coaches chose to visit.

Fundamentals

Without fail, on a daily basis, the classroom intercom phone would sound and Mrs. Snellenberger would answer it with a perturbed look, not hiding her displeasure at the interruption. A glance in my direction told me that my football coach was calling to let me know another college coach was in the athletic office, requesting my immediate presence. I sincerely felt that meetings with coaches named Schembechler, Paterno, Rogers, and Corso took precedence over Senior English. However, Mrs. Snellenberger was not impressed – nor would she acquiesce to my coach's request to be released early from class. Her standard response to these requests was polite, stern and consistent, "Yes, he is here, and I will have him report to the football office at the end of class."

    The tone of her response, body language and direct eye contact with me made it very clear: Her class took priority, an early dismissal was not an option, nor was it open for debate. Her refusal infuriated me; I was certain she was deliberately sabotaging my college and professional football career. The final minutes of class following these calls would drag on for what seemed like hours. And I'm happy to say that despite Mrs. Snellenberger's attempts to thwart my football career, I was offered and accepted a full scholarship to play for legendary coach Bo Schembechler at Michigan in late February 1980.

    One week before graduation, Mrs. Snellenberger asked me to stay after class for a few minutes to discuss something. I sincerely hoped it would be to commend me on the term paper I had spent the entire semester completing.

    She began our private conversation by congratulating me on my scholarship and wishing me all the best at Michigan. She then inquired as to my plans.

    "After college, it's my goal to play professional football," I replied.

She thought that was a noble plan, and once again wished me nothing but the best. However, she pressed on by asking me, "What are your plans for life after football?"

I must admit, I had not put a lot of thought into life after football.

Mrs. Snellenberger could tell by my lack of a response that I was clueless. She then changed the topic and asked whether I was aware why she refused to dismiss me early from class to meet with college coaches. I shared with her that I did not and that making the coaches and me wait was a source of great frustration.

She drew in a deep breath, then said that teaching to her was "more than just a job; it was her passion to ensure that all of her students possessed the necessary fundamental skills to be successful in any endeavor in life." It was as if she were reading my mind as she continued staring directly into my eyes. "These skills," she said, "are the ability to read, write and speak in front of groups."

At this point in my young life, I failed to share her passion and felt these "fundamental skills" she was referring to were just another hurdle to navigate in order to get me to the next level. That level being college, then the NFL. Mrs. Snellenberger continued by informing me that allowing an early departure from class would be not only an injustice to my classmates but also to me. I smirked, thinking that she had failed to grasp the urgency of my meeting these coaches. And I could have cared less that she was tasked with making certain these important skills were thoroughly engrained before I graduated from high school. However, she made it very clear that success in any endeavor would require a high level of skill in reading, writing and public speaking.

She implored me to take full advantage of the academic opportunities I would be offered at Michigan. She told me the education I would receive and the friendships I would make would be invaluable.

Mrs. Snellenberger couldn't have been more correct.

I still vividly remember this conversation 40 years later, and I am forever grateful that this caring and concerned teacher took the extra time and effort to impart this valuable life lesson, one that has benefitted me in my diverse career paths.

Senior English class, Alma High School, May 1980. Mrs. Snellenberger (far right in the window) trying to corral a bunch of 17- and 18-year-olds ready to go out and conquer the world. That's me in the front row!

What I've learned

1. Fundamentals are the basis of any successful endeavor.
2. Fundamentals should be considered an investment.
3. Adherence to fundamentals helps create patience.

What you can learn

- Although at times fundamentals may seem boring and monotonous, they cannot be overlooked and must be practiced until mastered.
- Mastering fundamentals will ensure success in any endeavor.
- You can have all the talent in the world, but if you fail to grasp the importance of fundamentals, you will never fulfill your potential.

Challenge question

What fundamental skills can you identify that if practiced—and mastered—would help you become more successful?

Bible verse

Proverbs 9:9 – "Instruct the wise and they will be wiser still; teach the righteous and they will add to their learning."

Postscript

Several years ago, Dawn and I joined a volunteer organization called "Read to a Child." It is a national lunchtime reading program in which an adult volunteer is paired with an at-risk elementary school student.

While the child eats lunch, the adult reads aloud one-on-one. This relationship lasts the entire school year and often extends for multiple years through the end of fourth grade.

Fundamentals

The simple act of reading aloud to a child once a week, over a period of time, has a profoundly positive impact on a child's future.

In 2021, Dawn and I completed our third year with the same children that were initially assigned to us. We are grateful for the awesome opportunity this has given us to invest in the lives of these children!

For more information about "Read to a Child," go to www.readtoachild.org. Trust me, it will change your life … and the life of an at-risk child.

CHAPTER 6
DREAM BIG

"You are one idea, one risk, one decision away from a totally different life. Of course, it'll probably be the toughest decision you ever make, the scariest risk you ever take. But if your dream doesn't scare you, it's too small."

– Mark Batterson

"If you got a dream, chase it, 'cause a dream won't chase you back."

– Cody Johnson

Dream: A strongly desired goal, aspiration or ambition.

Think back to when you were a child. Dreaming was something you did all the time. We dreamed of becoming a superhero, an astronaut, a world-class athlete, a rock star, and more.

Maybe you were one who held fast to your dreams and became who or what you dreamt. Or maybe you were one of the many who allowed negative people or circumstances to vanquish the thoughts, images or emotions that once brought a smile to your face.

    I genuinely believe that the ability to dream is a gift inherent in all of us; a gift that we must embrace, protect and cultivate during our lives. Dreaming big helps to steer us toward the areas of our giftedness and can serve as a template for goals that will lead us to success in whatever arena we so choose. Being the son and grandson of great athletes and coaches, I naturally had dreams of being a sports hero from an early age in my life. I have always had a love of sports, and big dreams and grandiose plans about where my athletic prowess would lead me. My family, friends, relatives, teachers and coaches have shared several humorous stories while recalling the dreams I boldly shared. One story comes from my eighth-grade home economics teacher, who taught a class called Bachelor's Groove. This class taught basic skills that all bachelors in the mid-1970s needed to possess: the finer points of ironing clothes, basic sewing skills, and, of course, the fundamentals of making the perfect grilled cheese sandwich. Four years later, after honing the skills I learned in Bachelor's Groove and countless grilled cheese sandwiches, I received a graduation card from the teacher. She included the note I had written on the first day on why I had chosen Bachelor's Groove: "I am going to be a pro football player, and I will need to know these things when I'm living on my own."

    I still smile when recalling this incident. I certainly wasn't afraid to share my dreams. And you must admit that, for a young man, I was focused on having a great future.

    It's unfortunate that in today's world, those who dream big are often ostracized and ridiculed. Who can calculate the number of dreams and dreamers negatively affected by the cynical attitudes of others?

Dream Big

Fortunately, those who encouraged me far outnumbered those who discouraged me when I shared my dreams. A major cultivator of my dreams was a big dreamer himself. Here's his story. Dave Arnold, my high school football coach, arrived in Alma, Michigan, in the early 1970s, not long before I entered high school. He was in his late 20s and came to my small town to revive a once proud program. He was a former college player who, after graduation, chose to pursue his dream as a high school, college and ultimately National Football League coach. My father, who was a teacher at Alma High School as well as a college football coach, was one of the first people who welcomed Coach Arnold to our community. My dad was thoroughly impressed with this enthusiastic, energetic young coach, and often told me how fortunate I was to have the opportunity to play for him. After assembling his staff, Coach Arnold went to work to change the culture of mediocrity that had infused our program. Coach Arnold's first and foremost task was teaching his staff and players how to set goals. His second and equally important task was teaching us the arduous process that would lead us to the successful completion of the goals we set.

He explained that goals must be specific, must be written out and must be displayed in a prominent location where they can be seen daily. He then challenged every coach and player to set individual goals for the upcoming season, had us write them down and then post them in our lockers. Once this was completed, he scheduled a meeting of all coaches and players in which we would establish our team goals for the season. I still recall our team's excitement and enthusiasm for implementing this formula as we sought to win our first conference championship in several years. Seeing my individual and our team goals each day created focus, tenacity and intensity that I had not experienced in my young life. The goals displayed in my locker served as the catalyst to keep the team and me focused and motivated through a season that would see us win a conference championship.

Looking back, the first goals I set seemed quite modest when compared to the goals I would set in the future. However, the confidence I acquired in this goal-setting process was something I have never forgotten and continue to implement to this day.

As a senior in high school, I set and achieved even bigger goals that helped earn an athletic scholarship. Prior to my first season as a Michigan Wolverine in the fall of 1980, I was introduced to yet another successful system to achieve big goals.

In a team meeting with 100 players and 20 staffers, head coach Bo Schembechler introduced us to a system that he used during his career to achieve individual and team success. He told us that the short-term and long-term goals we would set must be lofty enough to make us uncomfortable. He made it clear that the work we would be tasked with performing to achieve these goals would require us to withstand periods of great discomfort. He further explained that improvement required growth, and that growth came from doing things that required the mental and physical toughness that a vast majority of people were unwilling to muster.

Coach Schembechler challenged us individually and as a team to set big goals and be ready to work harder than we ever had to achieve these goals. He assured us that if we were willing to work hard, we would become a championship team.

The next step in this process was to write our individual goals, both academic and athletic, on two 3x5 cards that he provided to each player. He then told us to keep one card while he retained the duplicate.

Dream Big

Coach Schembechler's next challenge was to assist us in setting our team goals for the 1980 season. With senior team members providing most of the direction, we set goals that would require hard work, focus, tenacity and some old-fashioned good luck.

We were then given an additional card on which we were to write down our team goals. Lastly, Coach Schembechler handed out a blue bi-fold card wallet in which we were to keep our cards.

He then told us to carry these "goal notebooks" that contained both team and individual goals and refer to them often. The tone in his voice made it perfectly clear: This was an order, not an option.

The 1980 season started with a narrow victory followed by two losses. At 1-2, it was the worst start a Michigan team had had under Coach Schembechler. However, after some serious soul-searching by players and coaches, we went on to win nine consecutive games. We beat Ohio State in Columbus to win the Big Ten championship and earn a trip to the Rose Bowl. In Pasadena, we soundly defeated the Washington Huskies to give Coach Schembechler his first Rose Bowl victory.

In 1981, after spring practices were completed, each returning player had a meeting with Coach Schembechler. During these meetings, Coach removed his copy of our individual and team goals from our fall goal-setting meeting. Goals achieved were considered victories, and goals not achieved were considered losses. It was a simple yet extremely effective system for us to learn some great lessons. We learned how to win, and oftentimes, more importantly, we learned how to lose. He instilled in us that victories were to be built upon and losses were temporary and should be used as learning tools for the future.

During his career and until his death in 2006, Coach Schembechler was quoted in interviews and books as saying that he was not concerned about how many victories his players accumulated during their careers. He cared more about the types of husbands, fathers, friends and quality men of character and integrity that his players became after their playing days.

Coach Dave Arnold and I at my induction to the Alma High School Athletic Hall of Fame, 2013. I cannot thank this man enough for teaching me to "dream big."

What I've learned

1. If you dream it, you can achieve it.
2. Setting goals is the roadmap to achieving dreams.
3. Goal setting is a process that requires daily focus and effort.

What you can learn

- Pursuit of your dreams creates high levels of excitement and anticipation.
- Chasing your dreams with clearly defined goals will improve your ability to overcome adversity, challenges and limiting beliefs.
- Realization of your dreams equals success. Success will expand the level and scope of your influence.

Challenge question

What dream has been placed upon your heart that you have yet to act upon?

Bible verse

Ephesians 3:20 – "God can do anything, you know, far more than you could ever imagine, guess or request in your wildest dreams" (The Message Bible).

Postscript

My high school coach, Dave Arnold, left the prep ranks the summer before the 1980 season at Alma to become a graduate assistant at Michigan State University. Two years later, he was the offensive line coach at Montana State University. In 1983, he took over the Montana State program as head coach and promptly finished 1-10. The next season, his Bobcats went 12-2 and won the NCAA Division I-AA national championship.

In 1987, he joined Dennis Erickson's staff at Washington State University, then moved with him to the University of Miami (Florida), where the Miami Hurricanes won NCAA championships in 1989 and 1991. Finally, he followed Erickson to the NFL's Seattle Seahawks, where he served as the Special Teams Coordinator for three seasons.

Coach Arnold has since retired from full-time coaching. But, as of this writing, he can still be seen on the practice fields and sidelines at Northwood University, where his son E.J. is an assistant coach.

Thank you, Coach, for teaching me to dream big!

CHAPTER 7
LOOK SHARP

"Looking good isn't about self-importance; it's about self-respect."

– Charles Hix

Upon my graduation from the University of Michigan in 1986, I had to face two revelations. Number one, my football career was over, and number two, I was definitely not ready for nor prepared to join the workforce in pursuit of a "conventional career."

For the first time in my life, at 22 years of age, I found myself with neither a game plan nor a roadmap for the future. Coupled with moving back home with my parents (which was not met with joy), I was quite certain some important decisions needed to be made and made quickly.

During this period of soul searching, I did what all recent college graduates did in the mid-1980s. I sent out stacks of resumes loaded with letters of recommendation and waited for the phone to ring with a job offer. Fortunately for me, a family friend who had recently become a Special Agent with the Bureau of Alcohol, Tobacco and Firearms (ATF) invited me to the Detroit Field Office to check out what being a federal agent entailed.

I never fathomed myself working in law enforcement. However, I must admit I was intrigued and I felt a sense of excitement at the possibility of a new challenge.

After touring ATF headquarters in Detroit, I went to hang out (have drinks) with other federal, state and local law enforcement officers at a "cop friendly" watering hole in downtown Detroit. I thoroughly enjoyed meeting these people and was welcomed warmly because I was a friend of a current federal agent and a former Michigan football player. One agent I met provided some insight into what his unique view of a law enforcement career entailed. He shared with me that a career in law-enforcement allowed him to "prolong his adolescence." At that time, I found this humorous and over the course of my career and the passing of time quite insightful … and true.

Not being a believer in chance or coincidence, I now realize that the attraction and ultimately my decision to pursue this career path and the adventure, excitement and opportunities provided in this line of work were part of God's plan for my life.

The reaction from family and friends concerning my decision to become a federal agent was met with surprise, curiosity and hesitation as no member of my family had ever been in law enforcement.

However, at this point in my life, I was like a ship without a rudder on a stormy ocean. I needed a new challenge, a defined purpose, and most importantly, I needed to be part of a team again. Initially, I offered my services to the FBI only to be told that they weren't hiring college undergraduates who did not possess graduate degrees in accounting, law or foreign languages.

Look Sharp

I was advised to take my gung-ho attitude and my Bachelor of General Studies Degree, (the same degree that Jim Hackett, former Michigan football player and CEO of Ford Motor Company, and Jim Harbaugh, former Head Football Coach at the University of Michigan, possess) and offer my services to the United States Border Patrol. Even though I was unaware (as most people still are) of the duties performed by a Border Patrol Agent, I was immediately intrigued by this job prospect. My intrigue was raised even further after the FBI agent whom I spoke with informed me that the Border Patrol was the "Marine Corps" of federal law enforcement because of their lengthy, arduous and demanding academy and probationary period.

During my hiring interview with two Supervisory Border Patrol Agents that were serving in the Detroit Sector of the Border Patrol, stated they were impressed that I had a four-year degree from the University of Michigan; a majority of applicants had military and/or law enforcement backgrounds. They told me on several occasions that their academy was extremely challenging, both physically and mentally. This led me to believe that they were questioning my toughness. This also lit the competitive fire in me that had been dormant for the past few months and I responded with my usual bravado (at times this has been described as arrogance), "I've made it through four years at Michigan with Bo Schembechler, I'm confident that I can handle whatever you can throw at me."

They responded with blank expressions, and said nothing.

However, once the interview was over, they informed me I had successfully completed the oral and written requirements, was hired and told to wait for an appointment with the United States Border Patrol.

You're Allowed To Try

After an 18 month wait that challenged my limited patience threshold, I finally received an appointment to the 195th session of the United States Border Patrol Academy. My assigned duty post was to be in Douglas, Arizona, located in the Tucson Sector in rural southeastern Arizona on the Mexican border.

I arrived in Arizona on May 19, 1986 and a day later was sworn in as a Border Patrol Agent "Trainee" at the Tucson Sector Headquarters. Immediately following our "swearing in" my classmates (40 in total) received our badges and uniforms and were flown to Jacksonville, Florida. After collecting our luggage, we were then transported by bus an hour north to Glynco, Georgia, where the FLETC is located. This training base would be my home for the next six long, hot months.

As we approached our destination and home for the next six months, the excitement, anticipation and realization of this decision weighed heavily upon my classmates and me. During the drive north from Jacksonville to coastal Georgia, our driver informed us that we were to be "quartered" in "Animal House", the unofficial name of the dormitory that housed only trainees of the U.S. Border Patrol during basic training.

Upon entering the gates of the FLETC, I was immediately impressed at the size of this former Naval Air Station that had been converted into the world's largest law enforcement training center by the Carter Administration in the late 1970s.

I also couldn't help noticing the smirks on the faces of our driver and the FLETC rep who coordinated our arrival and check-in. As we pulled into the parking lot of "Animal House" we got a first glimpse of our home for the next six months. We hardly noticed the ugly, gray, concrete dormitory shaded by Georgia pines as our eyes were drawn to the two lines of rowdy, short-haired men on both sides of the sidewalk leading into our new residence.

As the bus door swung open, a young man from the many bodies lining the walk jumped on the bus and directed

Look Sharp

us to "get your asses off the bus." We grabbed our gear, exited the bus and were met with a shower of foamy beer and expletive filled greetings from members of the senior classes welcoming us to Border Patrol basic training.

This practice has been a time-honored tradition celebrating the arrival of a new class at the academy. As the beer shower ended, a young man came up to me, shook my hand, introduced himself as a member of the senior class, handed me a beer, grabbed my bags and led me to my assigned room.

From day one at the academy, I thrived on the highly disciplined structure of law-enforcement training. My days were filled with intensive instruction in the Spanish language (a requisite for all Border Patrol Agents), immigration law, firearms training, defensive and pursuit driving, defensive tactics and daily two-hour physical training sessions. It became apparent to me that I sorely missed the social structure and team environment that organized team sports offered. This environment not only challenged me, but also provided access to teammates, coaches, and officers that served as a source of constant motivation to "get better every day."

One of the several paramilitary rituals still practiced today by the Border Patrol Academy is the weekly uniform inspection of trainee agents and their respective classes every Monday morning at 7 am. Each agent and their class are inspected by the Chief Patrol Agent and the supervisory staff assigned to the academy. As the largest uniformed law enforcement agency in the United States, the Border Patrol maintains the highest levels of uniform and personal grooming standards. On a weekly basis, trainee agents are to have uniforms cleaned and neatly pressed, boots and brass shined to a mirror-like finish, hair neatly trimmed above the ears, and no trace of facial hair other than a neatly trimmed mustache is allowed. The majority of my classmates had served in the military before joining the Border Patrol and graciously helped this "college boy" prepare for these weekly inspections. I however, did not enthusiastically embrace this ritual and its attention to detail as much as my classmates. I felt that excelling in areas that I deemed more important, like academics, firearms training, and physical training, took precedence over mandatory uniform and grooming standards. I should have taken the advice of my classmates and the less-than-stellar comments from Border Patrol Supervisors concerning my uniform appearance, but I was too focused on the graded tests and the practical exercises that occurred on a daily basis.

One steamy morning in South Georgia, while standing at attention during our weekly uniform inspection, Supervisory Border Patrol Agent Mr. Paul Conover—the supervisory agent in charge of our class—instructed me to report to his office at the end of training. I could tell by the tone of his voice and his physical demeanor that a "coaching session" was in my future from a man who, unbeknownst to me, was a decorated veteran of the US Marine Corps, and a highly respected agent within the US Border Patrol. I reported to his office, was greeted cordially and told to "take a seat," while he glanced through my personnel file. It contained important information, including my education, employment history, and background check. Supervisory Agent Conover claimed he was impressed with my academic and athletic career while at the University of Michigan. He then looked up, stared directly at me and stated that "past success does not necessarily guarantee future success." He then asked me why I failed to demonstrate the same amount of pride in being

Look Sharp

a member of the United States Border Patrol that I had while I was a member of the Michigan Wolverine football team. Before I could respond, he told me it was more than obvious that "professional appearance," which was an important criterion for a uniformed officer, was not something I deemed important. He told me that my wrinkled uniform, scuffed boots and dull brass on my duty belt, coupled with my longer than regulation hair and razor stubble would no longer be tolerated.

In a moment of youthful arrogance immediately following Mr. Conover's critique, I almost blurred it out, "Are you serious?" Thank God I chose to remain silent! It became obvious to me that I had somehow convinced myself that maintaining and exhibiting a clean-cut, professional appearance was of lesser importance than the other graded elements necessary to graduate from the academy and become a Journeyman Patrol Agent.

Mr. Conover's demeanor softened slightly, and I realized the butt-chewing was over. He then shared some information I was unaware of that pertained to officer safety and survival. He stated that, "A professional appearance and demeanor demonstrated by an officer at the onset of a potentially dangerous encounter has a direct impact on the outcome." Meaning that an officer who exhibits a self-confident demeanor and professional appearance stands a greater chance to diffuse a dangerous, and/or deadly encounter, as opposed to an officer who does not demonstrate these traits. At this early stage in my federal law enforcement career, I had no idea how valuable this advice would be, and more importantly, this particular agent was a subject-matter expert in life and death situations.

Paul Conover joined the United States Marine Corps in 1968 and served our country in Vietnam. Shortly after his honorable discharge, he was appointed to the 121st session of the United States Border Patrol and was stationed in Presidio, Texas. Presidio is a rural outpost near Big Bend National Park in West Texas. This area was, and still is, a hotbed for human and narcotics smuggling on the Mexican border. On a broiling hot summer day in August 1982, Agent Conover received information that a notorious drug smuggler from Mexico, who was wanted in the United States, had ridden his horse across a shallow spot in the Rio Grande to perpetrate a crime on US soil. It was common knowledge to the agents working in the Presidio Station that this particular criminal, nicknamed "El Gato" (the Cat in Spanish), had boasted that he would shoot and kill a Border Patrol Agent, if afforded the opportunity.

As fate would have it, Agent Conover was assigned to patrol the same area in which El Gato illegally crossed the international border. While following some "signs" (tracks left by humans and/or animals), Agent Conover came face-to-face with El Gato, who was sitting in a lawn chair holding a carbine rifle. The command, "Don't move!" barely left Conover's mouth before El Gato fired several times, hitting Conover in both his legs. After falling to the ground, Agent Conover was able to fire five shots from his 12-gauge shotgun, four of which hit El Gato. However, in the heat of this fiery exchange, El Gato kept shooting. While attempting to evade the barrage of gunshots, Conover was able to roll off the trail, only to be hit by a final round that went through his buttocks, perforated his colon, and lodged against his lower spine.

As the gun smoke cleared, Conover realized he was severely wounded and would need immediate medical care to survive. Fortunately, his partner was nearby and heard the exchange, and had already radioed for help.

The next several hours were a living nightmare for Agent Conover, but to this day, he is eternally grateful to be alive. It seemed if something could go wrong, it did. On the

90-mile journey to the nearest hospital, the "new" ambulance that was dispatched to the gunfight location overheated and broke down. However, good fortune was on Conover's side, and he was quickly moved to the Border Patrol Suburban that was serving as an escort.

Once underway, the transporting officers received instructions that emergency plans had been implemented. Unfortunately, the medical facility they were en route to was not equipped to treat Conover's injuries. They were instructed to meet a private pilot in a single-engine aircraft at a remote location to transport Conover to the United States Military Hospital at Fort Bliss in El Paso, Texas. After arriving at the airstrip, they loaded Conover into the small aircraft and continued on their journey to El Paso, a mere 250 miles (I cannot imagine the pain and discomfort Conover must have felt!). Nine-and-a-half hours after the gunfight a semiconscious Conover was wheeled into surgery.

After several more surgeries, extended hospital stays, and arduous physical rehabilitation, Agent Conover was deemed fit for duty and was assigned to the Duty Station in Presidio, Texas. Shortly thereafter, he was promoted to Supervisory Patrol Agent and was sent to the United States Border Patrol Academy, where I had the good fortune to have this "American hero" as my class coordinator, supervisor, leader, and mentor during my time as a Border Patrol Trainee.

Once again, as fate would have it, it was only a day or two after my "coaching session" with Agent Conover concerning my less-than-professional appearance that the ordeal endured by this man was shared with my classmates and me in an emotional, two-hour lecture given by this man himself. Conover gave us prudent advice on many topics, and I still recall one that stood out that day. He told us that we had chosen a very dangerous and unpredictable career, and we were never certain if we would return home safely after each shift.

You're Allowed To Try

He shared a heartfelt story about what he was thinking about while being prepped for surgery after the gun fight. All he was thinking about was the disagreement he and his wife had the night before, and he neglected to kiss her goodbye and tell her that he loved her. As I glanced around the room at my classmates, I noticed quite a few of my "rough-and-tumble" future federal agents had tear-filled eyes.

Needless to say, the transparency displayed by Conover created a level of credibility that led all of us to heed his advice and teachings, all of which helped us become better law enforcement officers and better men.

From that day forward, I have always made it a priority to portray a professional appearance and demeanor during my interactions with all people whom I come into contact with.

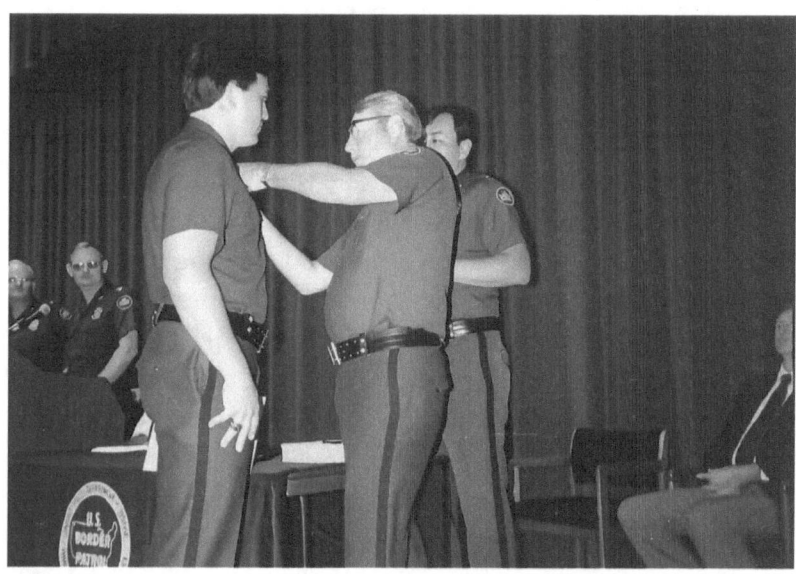

Badge pinning ceremony on graduation day from the United States Border Patrol Academy, September 1986. Serving as a United States Border Patrol agent has been one of my greatest honors.

Look Sharp

 Police Training Class #17PI-606/195
Border Patrol Academy
Federal Law Enforcement Training Center
May 23, 1986 - September 24, 1986
Glynco, Georgia

This is a class photo of the 195th session of the United States Border Patrol Academy. Our class motto was, "MEAN GREEN 1-9-5, THE TRAINING'S TOUGH, THE STRONG SURVIVE."

Supervisory Border Patrol Agent, Paul Conover, is sitting in the 5th chair from the right in the front row. Border Patrol Agent "Trainee" Lawrence "Jake" Sweeney is proudly sitting in the 1st chair from the left.

What I've learned

1. Looking good shows respect for yourself and others.
2. Looking good makes you feel better.
3. Looking good shows pride in appearance and adds to a person's professional demeanor.

What you can learn

- Dressing well and being well groomed is proven to increase your self-confidence.
- Looking professional demonstrates that you take the time and effort to show respect for the people in your workplace or the people you serve.
- A sharp appearance shows you care about yourself and take pride in your profession.

Challenge question

How are you "looking the part" in your work world? At church? With your family? And most important, with God? Are you showing up as the real you, or as a facade?

Bible verse

Ester 5:1 – "On the third day Esther put on her royal robes and stood in the inner court of the palace, in front of the king's hall." (NIV)

Postscript

The criminal alien, drug, gun and human smuggler, "El Gato" managed to evade capture immediately following the gun fight with Agent Conover by crawling through the thick brush on the banks of the Rio Grande. There, he was able to locate some of his "compadres" who took him to have his gunshot wounds treated at a hospital in Pecos, Texas. He was arrested and confined under guard at the hospital. This, however, did not stop his compadres from attempting an unsuccessful escape from captivity while recovering.

Following his recovery, El Gato was tried in federal court, where Agent Conover testified against him. He was found guilty and sentenced to the maximum-security ward at the United States Penitentiary in Leavenworth, Kansas. Upon his parole, he was formally deported from the United States and later killed in a gun battle in Ojinaga, Chihuahua, Mexico.

CHAPTER 8
THE VALUE OF HARD WORK

> "Success is no accident. It is hard work, perseverance, learning, studying, sacrifice and most of all, love of what you are doing or learning to do."
>
> – Pelé

For the first eighteen years of my life, I lived in a small town. Oftentimes, I hear people say they "grew up" in a small town. However, I choose to say, "I'm from a small town," because, after six decades, I still feel that I have yet to grow up. I have come to realize that the process of growing up continues from birth until death.

Prior to departing for college, my family lived in Alma, Michigan. Alma was incorporated as a village in 1872 and became a city in 1905. Alma's main industries are manufacturing, healthcare and agriculture. It is home to Alma College, a private liberal arts college with an enrollment of 1,400. Alma also has one public high school, of which I am a proud member of the 1980 graduating class.

My parents were offered employment opportunities in Alma in the early 1960s, shortly after my birth in 1962. My father, Michael Sweeney, was hired as the head football coach at Alma High School also serving as an art teacher. My mother, Bonnie, was a registered nurse and was hired as the Assistant Director of Nursing at the Michigan Masonic Home, a large geriatric facility that still operates in Alma. A short time after she began her employment, she was promoted to Director of Nursing and held that position for 30 years, until her retirement.

I was raised as an only child in what is now referred to as a "dual-career" household, since both my parents were members of the labor force who worked outside of our home.

In my early years, I assumed all families had the same dual-career situation that I was fortunate to grow up in. My mother worked from 7 a.m. until 3 p.m., Monday through Friday, and my father had a similar schedule as a teacher.

Some of my earliest memories include listening to my parents talk about the goals they had for themselves; goals that, in order to achieve them, would require strategic planning, sacrifice and hard work. At that time, I had no idea I was seeing the value and benefits of hard work modeled by my parents at an early age.

Early in their marriage, my parents made a purposeful decision to purchase a vacation home on a lake in northeastern Michigan, prior to buying a home in the city where they resided and worked. On several occasions later in my life, before the passing of both my parents, I recall stories of the "blowback" they received from their respective parents concerning the "reckless and emotional" decision to purchase a vacation home so early in their marriage and careers.

The next "reckless" decision my parents made shortly after purchasing their "cottage" (vacation home) was to purchase not one, but two houses directly adjacent to the campus of Central Michigan University. Coincidentally, these houses were located on the same street where my father was raised in Mt. Pleasant, Michigan, a city 20 miles north of Alma.

The Value Of Hard Work

My parents' plan was to renovate these houses and rent them to college students as an extra source of income. I was eight years old, and I can recall lengthy discussions between my parents concerning the time, effort and resources it would require before this income stream would materialize. A majority of these discussions were held on car rides to our vacation home, which my father would refer to as the "cabin."

My parents agreed that the extra resources necessary for the rental house project would be provided by my father. He opted to resign his position as Alma High School's head football coach and accepted a new position as an assistant football coach at Alma College. He did this while remaining a full-time teacher at Alma High School.

Since Alma College is an NCAA Division III sports program, their respective sports programs are not year-round. The opportunity to coach additional sports at Alma College and make more money to finance his rental project became a viable option, and he accepted the position of head tennis coach at Alma College. A short time after, a close friend, who happened to be the head basketball coach at Alma College, needed an assistant coach and offered that position to my father. He readily accepted and was now coaching three college sports in addition to being a full-time public-school teacher.

My father's work ethic, energy level and self-discipline exceeded a level that I rarely see today. In retrospect, I now see that this was possible because of his passion and love for teaching and coaching, as well as his desire to provide a better life for his family.

During my childhood, my father would leave for his teaching duties at 7:30 a.m. and return home at 2:30 p.m. to grab a short 15-minute nap and a quick cup of coffee before heading to practice sessions and/or games (depending on the season). If possible, he would return home around 6:30 p.m.

and have dinner with my mother and I before heading 20 miles north to Mt. Pleasant to maintain and renovate his rental houses, or as they're now referred to as investment properties, until around midnight most nights. He continued this rigorous schedule for several years without complaint.

I had the great pleasure of accompanying my father to countless practice sessions and games before I began my athletic career. I witnessed firsthand his passion for coaching, mentoring and motivating college athletes to become better players, team members and young men. He possessed an innate ability to show players not how far they had to go to become champions, but to embrace and enjoy the process that can oftentimes include, hard work, discomfort, injury and the disappointment of losing. A few years later, I would learn that these skills are a gift that all great coaches want to bestow on their athletes.

Most people are unaware that Division III athletes do not receive athletic scholarships to play for their colleges. Instead, they choose to participate in sports for the enjoyment of the game. They differ from Division I scholarship athletes, like my grandfather, father and me, who were basically "employees" of their respective university athletic departments.

I share this information with you to further explain my father's skill as a college coach. He had an uncanny ability to recruit great athletes to play on his teams for the "love of the game", while the athletes and/or the athlete's parents paid for their education at this small, private and expensive liberal arts college.

I now fully understand his decision to remain at Alma College, even though he was offered the opportunity to serve as a Division I coach during his career. He chose to spend more time with his family while away from his teaching and coaching duties during the spectacular northeastern Michigan summers.

I am forever grateful to both my parents for modeling the importance of hard work and the satisfaction and benefits derived from following my passions and serving others.

Mike and Bonnie Sweeney are now both deceased. My mother passed away after a lengthy illness in December 2022. My father passed away in 2011 in his sleep at his favorite place on earth, his "cottage" in northeastern Michigan. This was the same cottage my parents purchased as a young married couple in May of 1962, against the wishes of their parents.

Prior to my mother's passing, she informed my wife and I that she and my father had legal documents drawn up that would name us as the deeded owners of their vacation home after her death. The only stipulation was that the property would remain in the Sweeney family and would be handed down to my children as a place of rest, relaxation, and celebration.

My dad, Mike Sweeney, relaxing on the "boathouse deck" overlooking beautiful Hubbard Lake in northeastern Michigan.

What I've learned

1. There is no substitute for hard work.
2. Hard work builds character.
3. Superior talent without a work ethic to match is useless.

What you can learn

- Hard work always results in something positive.
- The harder you work, the greater the opportunities you'll have.
- Hard work creates character and discipline, and there is no substitute for either of these.

Challenge question

Who can you identify that you consider to be extremely successful, and how can you find out how hard they worked to get where they're at?

Bible verse

Proverbs 14:23 – "There is profit in hard work, but mere talk leads to poverty."

CHAPTER 9
COMMIT TO FINISH

"You Can't Finish What You Don't Start, and You Should Never Start What You're Not Committed to Finish"

– Gary Ryan Blair

Commitment: An agreement or pledge to do something in the future.

To the best of my recollection, I fell in love with sports at around eight years of age. Like many small-town boys, I started playing baseball and was good enough to make the Pee Wee League All-Star game my first season. However, one of my first and last baseball memories was striking out as the last batter in that game. It was my first bitter taste of losing in team sports. That single event may have led me into a sport that I grew to love as a young athlete. A sport that I still love today: Tennis.

It was evident that I had a gift for this individual sport shortly after I learned the game on the public courts at a park in my hometown. A couple years later, after some lessons and hours of hitting off a backboard at this same park, I had become an accomplished youth player.

You're Allowed To Try

From the age of ten until my graduation from high school, my parents would send me to tennis camp for two weeks every summer. The purpose was twofold: first and foremost, to hone my skills, and second, to compete against other talented junior players from around the Midwest.

My father selected these camps based upon the coaching skills and the reputations of the coaches and/or camp directors that conducted them. Initially, I did not see the coincidence of these coaches also being rival coaches that his Alma College teams competed against on an annual basis.

Attending camps each summer while in junior high and high school allowed me the opportunity to play against great junior players and to be coached by several All-American college players, as well as legendary coach George Acker, who was the Head Tennis Coach at Kalamazoo College, Michigan. This iconic coach ran the tennis program from 1958 to 1993. He coached the team to 35 consecutive MIAA Conference Championships and seven NCAA Division III National Championships.

During my middle school years, in the weeks immediately following my camp attendance, my father would take me around the state of Michigan to play in junior tournaments. In virtually all of these tournaments, my father made me "play up," which means I would compete in a higher age bracket than my actual age. Each week, I would hold onto the false hope that he would allow me to compete against players my age, but he steadfastly refused. His reply never wavered: "You're not here to collect trophies, you're here to improve." I did improve; however, there were some tough losses and lessons to be learned.

As a former athlete and a current coach, I can assure you that you learn much more in defeat than you do in victory. This is a major coaching point I share with all the athletes I work with. I tell each person that I can still list the opponents and remember the margin of defeat in the games the Michigan Wolverines lost while I was a player from 1980-1983.

Commit To Finish

Competing against older opponents, who were more physically developed, helped to make me a much better player and also helped me acquire a higher degree of mental toughness and resiliency that would serve me throughout my life.

Shortly after a successful season during my first year of high school tennis, I highly anticipated another couple of weeks at tennis camp to further hone my skills. However, I began to experience continual and sharp pains in my right elbow, the same arm I used to swing my racket. I was about to experience the first significant injury of my athletic career. The injury proved devastating to my family and me, and it set in motion a chain of events that would provide one of the greatest life lessons I could ask for.

After visits with two orthopedic surgeons, it was determined that my right elbow has sustained severe joint damage and that a surgical repair would not fix the problem. The doctor told my parents and me that my tennis career was over. Needless to say, I was devastated; my goal of being a Division I NCAA player and possibly playing professionally had come to an end.

After a period of emotional mourning on my part, my father and I decided to pursue football as the path to college and the professional ranks. This new goal allowed me to focus on the future and move beyond my disappointment and sense of loss.

With my renewed focus, I began a conditioning program to prepare me for the upcoming football season. Soon after my change in athletic direction, my father asked me to sit down with him at our kitchen table. I knew something was up; this had always been the location for highly important discussions in the Sweeney family.

After we were both seated, he asked the following question: "Why not switch hands and play tennis with your left hand?" I was surprised that I had not thought of this. However, a few seconds later, I felt an almost overwhelming sense of dread when I considered the time and effort this initiative would take. I now fully recognize that this emotional, fear-based response is normal when a person sets a goal that is extremely challenging.

My father enthusiastically added that he had always noticed a skill that I possessed (and I had taken for granted): my ability to write my name, draw, throw and catch with both hands. I was then, and continue to be, what is termed ambidextrous. Ambidexterity is the ability to use both the right and left hands equally well. Only about 1 percent of the population is ambidextrous.3

Even though I was born with this trait, I knew that attempting to play at the level I was accustomed to would be extremely challenging. However, I was intrigued, and the initial dread I felt over the prospect of changing hands was gone. I was ready to give this a try because I sincerely missed playing tennis on a regular basis.

My father continued, telling me this would not be easy. He said I could hit my forehand stroke with my left hand and use a modified two-handed backhand stroke that was becoming commonplace in the 1970s. This would eliminate any undue stress on my injured right elbow, which to this day I am unable to straighten fully.

After making the decision to move forward with this new challenge, my father asked if I was totally committed to giving this my best effort and if I was willing to invest the time and hard work required. He said that quitting was not an option and that we all would have to make some sacrifices to make this happen. He asked if I was willing to miss time with friends and adhere to a rigorous schedule that he would oversee. He then added that our goal would be to enable me to play at the same level I was accustomed to in less than one year. I would set my sights on regaining my position as the number one singles player on my high school team. The only difference was that I would play my second season as a left-hander.

After a brief pause to consider this daunting task, I nodded in agreement. He then said words that I have never forgotten: "I need you to commit to this and finish it." I gave him my word that I would commit and finish. Quitting was not an option with my father once a commitment was made. Our meeting was over. It was time for both of us to go to work.

When we arrived at the facility for my next scheduled practice session, my father informed me that he had hired a professional to personally direct the remainder of my tennis training. This coach worked with me on the physical aspects of the game and also the mental aspects, which included visualization techniques that all great players use and practice to become consistent winners.

In the early winter of 1977, my dad and I put our plan into action. We drove two times per week to the nearest indoor tennis facility, 50 miles away in Bay City, Michigan, for a two-hour practice session. This was in addition to me running at least three miles on the nights we did not have practice. My father explained that my new style of play would require me to possess a higher degree of physical conditioning.

The initial practices were more difficult than I had envisioned. However, I was learning how to physically train my body. I realized that being able to withstand temporary unease, including aches and soreness, is a necessary component of improvement, both physically and mentally. After surviving the first few sessions, I began to improve at a rate that surprised not only my father and me, but also Chuck Brainard, the tennis professional who was in charge of managing and coaching at the indoor facility we had chosen for my training.[4]

You're Allowed To Try

The rewards from committing to this difficult challenge during my first winter of training were astounding! I upset the number one seeded player in our high school's conference tennis tournament and was the new conference champion—while playing left-handed.

I went on to win another conference singles championship my senior season, was elected team captain, and helped guide our team to an undefeated season and a conference championship. My Alma Panther teammates, in this tournament, won all seven flights (four singles and three doubles).

After my high school graduation, I left competitive tennis to pursue collegiate football. To this very day, the memories of my years as a tennis player bring a smile to my face whenever I reminisce about the challenges I faced, the lessons I learned and the great coaches, players and friends I made along the way.

All this would not have been possible if I had not made the decision to "commit and finish."

Chuck Brainard, tennis professional, helped my transition from right-handed player to left-handed.

What I've learned

1. Commitment is the path to achieving your goals.
2. Commitment encourages resilience in the face of adversity.
3. Commitment will boost self-confidence.

What you can learn

- Being committed will help develop new skills and keep you on track.
- Committed people serve as an inspiration for others.
- Commitment enhances accountability because it enhances "ownership".

Challenge question

When was the last time you committed to a goal and what was the result?

Bible verse

Proverbs 16:3 – "Commit your works to the Lord, and your plans will be established."

Postscript

1 https://www.apa.org/monitor/2009/01/brain

Chuck Brainard was born and raised in Hamtramck, Michigan. Hamtramck is a blue-collar suburb of Detroit and was once the home of several state, local, and national tennis champions who were coached and mentored by the famous tennis coach, Jean Hoxie.

Chuck was a two-time Michigan high school state champion and was named "Athlete of the Year" at Hamtramck High, prior to accepting a scholarship to Michigan State University

("MSU"). At MSU, he was a two-time Big Ten Champion and was recently named to the MSU All Century Tennis Team.

After graduation, Chuck continued to compete and coach on a professional level and was the tennis professional and club manager at Bay Valley Tennis Club in Bay City, Michigan. He continues to play tennis every chance he gets and remains highly competitive.

After reconnecting with Chuck for this project, I asked him if he, like most aging tennis players, had taken up pickle ball. He laughed heartily and responded, "I plan on taking up that game when I turn 80."

CHAPTER 10
THE BENEFITS OF BEING COACHABLE

*"My best skill was that I was coachable.
I was a sponge and aggressive to learn."*

– Michael Jordan

Coachable: You're willing to accept the fact that there's something you have not yet learned, nor accomplished, that could make you better.

I would be less than truthful if I did not admit that my life has been a long journey, where learning to be coachable was not something I excelled at. In fact, as I look back, I was downright BAD at being coachable! However, as I tell my clients, "You've got to be bad before you're good." I'm quite certain that my life and the trials and tribulations that were all part of "growing up" and becoming mature would have been far less painful had I learned to be coachable at an earlier age.

I don't need to spend much time recalling some memorable examples of excellent coaching that were communicated to me. Unfortunately for me, a large percentage of valuable lessons I was offered were immediately disregarded—although some I actually considered, albeit briefly, before disregarding—and a few I actually accepted in an effort to improve.

Here are a few coaching points that have stayed with me.

- From one of my high school coaches who saw my potential, was aware of my aspirations and cared about my future:

    "If you don't stop hanging around with the crew you're running with, you'll just be another guy from here that could've been great."

- From my father, a college coach who was concerned I would be too fat and/or slow to be a college athlete. (He gave me this advice before the origins of "eating disorders" were fully understood):

    "You need to stop overeating, or you're going to eat yourself right out of your job in athletics."

- Advice given to me by one of my high school teachers and reiterated to me by an English professor at the University of Michigan:

    "Reading, writing, and public speaking are basic skills necessary to be successful in all future endeavors."

- From a college coach on my first full contact practice as a freshman:

    "You're going to have to give 100 percent effort in practice if you want to play here. Practice is where you earn the privilege to play in the Big Ten."

- From an instructor at the FLETC while I was in basic training at the US Border Patrol Academy:

The Benefits Of Being Coachable

> "What you have done in the past has no bearing on how successful you will be in the future."

- From a respected veteran US Border Patrol Agent after I told him that "experience was overrated," while I was applying for a supervisory position in federal law enforcement:

> "You'll never be a good leader until you learn to understand, value, and respect what you get from 'experience.'"

Remembering these specific instances demonstrates that, at some point, I had actually accepted and implemented these valuable coaching facts.

For me, the learning process wasn't easy, short, or pain-free. However, over the course of time and the lessons learned through experiencing successes and failures, I have come to value the benefits of learning how to accept coaching with an open mind. I have realized that I am not the smartest person in the room—even when I'm the only person in the room—and I can benefit from sound advice given by someone who genuinely cares about me and has achieved the level of success that I aspire to.

There are countless other tidbits of wisdom I've been given over the years, but one instance in particular sticks out among them all.

While vacationing on the Hawaiian Island of Maui, one of my favorite places, with my wife and some of her business peers, I was offered some "life advice" that, at the time, I didn't receive for its intended purposes. In retrospect, these words of wisdom were meant to make me a better person and an example to the people I have relationships with as a husband, father, coach, business person, leader and friend. Instead of heeding the advice, I chose to go back to my old ways of receiving coaching, which I call "offend and defend." I would be offended by the advice that was given and then defend my actions and behavior.

The unique components of this specific life advice, which I now refer to as coaching, was in the message and the messenger. I will first introduce you to the messenger:

Kathy Helou is a retired Elite Executive Senior National Sales Director with Mary Kay Cosmetics. She was, and remains, an iconic business leader with the largest color, skin care and cosmetics company in the United States. She shattered several company sales records as both a sales consultant and sales director—some still stand today, long after her retirement—and has earned over $20 million in commissions during her career.

Kathy's leadership and coaching skills have positively impacted countless individuals during her 38-year career, and have helped women become better business women, better wives and mothers, and leaders in their communities. The positive impact she has made on the people she has encountered is immeasurable.

In my opinion, her greatest attribute as a leader is her ability to give all the credit for the blessings she has received in her life and her business to the Lord. It is unfortunate that in our society, oftentimes, when a person proclaims they have a relationship with Jesus Christ through the teachings found in the Bible, they are ostracized.

Kathy is bold, yet sensitive in her "witness" and is unashamed to share the benefits she strongly feels that everyone can have through a relationship with her savior, Jesus Christ. The example that she has set in her life and business served as the motivation for my wife (who accompanied Kathy on

The Benefits Of Being Coachable

a trip to Paris in the early 1990s) to turn her life over to Jesus Christ. This life-changing decision ultimately led me to follow her lead a short time later.

Here are the events that led up to my conversation with Kathy and the "life advice" I received from this special person.

One evening, early on in my vacation to Hawaii, I was having an informal conversation with Kathy about my career as a Federal Law Enforcement Officer. She listened intently as I regaled several tales from my time on the Mexican border and my current assignment as a Supervisory Immigration Officer (until I left government service in 1996).

Of course, as I was regaling these tales, I added several expletives, as was my habit (albeit a bad one) that I grew accustomed to and had allowed to go unchecked for decades. Looking back, I should have noticed and acknowledged the look of disdain on her face as she listened to my tales. However, I chose to forge ahead, thinking that my "colorful" language was a necessary component of my informal conversations with people.

The next morning, while having breakfast alone at the hotel that Dawn and I were staying at, I was greeted by none other than Kathy Helou, who now held the esteemed position of Elite Executive Senior National Sales Director, the penultimate position with Mary Kay Cosmetics. A position of high esteem that was earned, not appointed. In her new position, she was tasked with mentoring, training and motivating business women from across the United States and several countries abroad. Being in a position of leadership, I could certainly respect her title, the responsibilities it held, and the hard work it took to achieve her position.

Kathy began by telling me how proud she was of my wife's achievements thus far in her career with Mary Kay Cosmetics and how honored she was to have the two of us as friends. She felt it would certainly be a lot of fun as we traveled the world together on incentive trips we could earn with this great company. I joked with her that, to my knowledge, the federal government was not sending me on any luxury trips for my hard work. We shared a good laugh ... but that's where the laughter ended.

She asked me if she could share something with me that had been weighing on her heart and that she had put prayerful consideration into. Not having any idea what might come of this, I agreed somewhat anxiously to hear her out.

I have to mention that this lady is a great and gifted communicator, but there was no sugar coating her words and the message she had chosen to share with me. She said she was shocked and disappointed to see a man of my stature and position, not to mention one who was a Christian and follower of Jesus Christ, use profanity so casually and without consideration for those around me. As with most of these types of conversations—and times when constructive criticism, or what I now refer to as coaching, is being offered—I was immediately offended and went on the defensive. I was quick to downplay my words and attempted to blame my unacceptable, rude, totally uncalled for, and habitual use of profanity, saying, "You don't understand; where I come from, I've been an athlete my whole life, and now I'm in law enforcement. That's just part of who I am."

Kathy met my defensive attitude with kind and insightful words of advice. She stated that my use of profanity, especially using the Lord's name in vain, was not what someone in my position—a husband, a father, a leader in my profession and especially a Christian—should continue to do. She added that it was not in line with who she knew me to be, and using profanity had a negative effect on my leadership skills and my Christian witness to other men and women who hold me in high esteem.

Before I could make further excuses and make myself look even worse, Kathy shared some scripture verses that dealt

The Benefits Of Being Coachable

with careless words and the power they have.[2] I had read these verses, but I must admit I had not considered the negative impact and image I had portrayed when using profane words on a regular basis.

From that day forward, I had made two very important decisions: Number one, that I stop using profanity. Number two, I had the humility to apologize for my rudeness and to thank Kathy for taking a relational risk by having this conversation.

It took a period of time to self-reflect and allow the seeds of this coaching session to take root. Being able to listen without becoming defensive is something that has taken me a long time to learn. Today, I look at this process as optimistically as I can, and I'm forever grateful that I have matured and learned how to take the sage advice of those who care about me. I strive daily to be the man that God created me to be.

Elite Executive Senior National Sales Director Kathy Helou and National Sales Director Dawn Otten-Sweeney. Great coaches don't always lead sports teams. These two coaches led championship sales teams.

What I've learned

1. When being "coached," you may not like what you hear.
2. Listen intently to what is being shared.
3. Take time to reflect and don't get emotional.

What you can learn

- Seek advice from those you respect and have achieved success.
- Seek clarity if you are not certain what is being conveyed.
- Apply what has been shared if it can make you better.

Challenge question

Who has been a coach for you in the past, and what lessons did you or could you learn?

Bible verse

Proverbs 19:20 – "Listen to advice and accept instruction that you may gain wisdom in the future."

Postscript

Having learned how to eat "humble pie" and to be coachable over the years, I've had the privilege of coaching many excellent student-athletes, and I'm so proud of their accomplishments in sports and in life!

2 Colossians 3:8 – "But now you put them all away: anger, wrath, malice, slander and obscene talk from your mouth."

Ephesians 4:29 – "Let no corrupting talk come out of your mouths, but only such is good for building up, as fits the occasion, that it may give grace to those who hear."

CHAPTER 11
AN ATTITUDE OF GRATITUDE

"Great things happen to those who don't stop believing, trying, learning, and being grateful."

– Roy T. Bennett

Gratitude: The quality of being thankful; readiness to show appreciation for and to return kindness.

I often reflect on how fortunate I have been throughout my life to have had so many people who have had a profound impact on my life. It warms my heart to recall the times I've spent with these special individuals. They were sincerely interested in imparting life lessons, often unintentionally, to me as a young man. Their success in life, business, and relationships caused me to pause and listen, even if I didn't take their sage advice at that time. In my younger days, this list was composed of those individuals who were ever present in my world: teachers, coaches, college athletes and counselors at sports camps

I attended. I would be remiss if I neglected to add my parents, grandparents, aunts and uncles (who also happened to be teachers, coaches and counselors).

One of the life lessons I'm referring to was imparted to me on the day prior to the 1983 Rose Bowl. We, the Big Ten Champion Michigan Wolverines, were slated to play the PAC 10 Champion UCLA Bruins the following day in the 69th Annual Rose Bowl on New Year's Day. This would be the second Rose Bowl game I would be playing in during my college career.

After our team's brief practice session—something that was the norm on the day before a game—the coaches gave us a few minutes to walk around the field, snap some photos (before camera phones) and take in the vast beauty and history found in this famous sports venue.

The Rose Bowl Stadium is about the same size and has a very similar shape and seating capacity as our home field, the famous Michigan Stadium in Ann Arbor. So similar, in fact, that many former Michigan football players refer to the Rose Bowl as "Big House West." However, that is where the similarities end. The Southern California landscape surrounding the Rose Bowl is breathtaking, to say the least. Palm trees can be seen above the rim of the stadium, with a view of snowcapped mountains in the background. Warm winds and temperatures in the 70s, coupled with low humidity, make for an almost surreal environment for a college football game to be played.

My roommates and I grabbed a seat on what was to be our sideline bench the next day to take in the sunset over the rim of the stadium, when one of our coaches joined us and began reminiscing about playing on this same field against the UCLA Bruins in the 33rd Rose Bowl in 1947. To this day, listening to this coach reminisce about his playing days four decades prior in this same stadium remains one of my fondest memories.

Here is his story.

Coach Alex Agase was introduced to the Michigan football team at our first full team meeting at the onset of the 1982 season, coincidentally a season that our team won a second Big Ten Championship during my four-year career.

Coach Schembechler introduced "Coach Ag," as we would soon refer to him, as a great coach, player, friend and war hero. This was 1982, less than ten years after the end of the Vietnam War. The "conflict", as it is commonly referred to, remains an unpleasant memory in American history. It was not common to hear someone introduced as a war hero during this era. I knew I had heard his name before, but I couldn't recall a time or place.

Coach Agase left college coaching in the late 1970s and had recently served as the Director of Athletics at Eastern Michigan University in nearby Ypsilanti. Coach Schembechler was ecstatic to have this knowledgeable and experienced man serving on his staff as a volunteer assistant. Coach "AG", as we referred to him, would work predominantly with the special teams, of which I played an integral part as the center on punts, field goals and extra points.

On one of my regular calls with my parents, shortly after that team meeting, I shared this information with my father, who was amazed that I would have the opportunity to be coached by Alex Agase. My dad referred to Coach AG as a "legend," referring to his collegiate and professional playing career as well as his coaching career. He did not, however, mention his military career, which I would soon hear about.

Alex Agase grew up in Illinois and attended the University of Illinois. While playing offensive guard, he was named All-American in 1942. After his first All-American season, he entered the United States Marine Corps and began his military training at Purdue University. During his training, he also played football for Purdue and was named All-American for a second time in 1943, helping the Boilermakers win the 1943 Big Ten Championship before his Marine Corps deployment.

While serving in the Marine Corps, Agase was deployed, along with thousands of other Marines, to the Pacific Theater of World War II to battle the Imperial Japanese Army in two of the fiercest battles in our country's history.

The battles of Iwo Jima and Okinawa are famous for their ferocity. Iwo Jima is a volcanic island in the Pacific Ocean and is only eight square miles, but the battle itself lasted five weeks and was defended by 18,000 Japanese soldiers, of whom only 216 were taken captive after the battle. The US Marines sustained over 26,000 casualties and 6,822 deaths.[4] The fighting on Okinawa was even fiercer. The Battle of Okinawa lasted 82 days and saw over 110,000 Japanese soldiers killed in action. The Allied Forces suffered 51,000 casualties and 12,513 deaths.[5]

Coach Agase was one of the Marine casualties on Okinawa and received a Purple Heart Medal for injuries sustained in combat.

After healing up, Agase returned to the University of Illinois for the 1946 season, where he earned All-American honors for the third time, and led his team to the 1947 Rose Bowl Championship in Pasadena, California.

After his collegiate career, Agase was drafted by the Cleveland Browns and was a key player on three NFL Championship teams. After retiring from professional football, he held head coaching positions at Northwestern University and Purdue University. One of his collegiate coaching highlights came in 1976 while coaching at Purdue. Coach Agase's unranked Boilermakers defeated the number 1 ranked Michigan Wolverines 16-14 in West Lafayette, Indiana.

    I remember the evening on the last day of 1982 so vividly that I can almost smell the fresh cut Bermuda/Rye grass that adorns the playing surface (and is replaced each year prior to the game being played). The look in Coach AG's eyes and the sound of his voice told us that he had mentally taken himself back to one of his finest victories and fondest memories as a college player. We could actually feel how grateful he was to recount this story and to have had the opportunity to play in this historic game. He remembered the exact score, the weather that afternoon, and even the slope of the field in the center to aid in the draining of water in the event of rain. While recalling this story, he harkened back to his Marine corps days in 1945 when fighting alongside his fellow marines in the South Pacific. He wasn't certain if he would make it home alive, let alone be able to play football again.

    I was certainly unaware of the ferocity of the enemy he faced and the carnage he had seen and survived during his wartime deployment. Only later, after I had read several books that graphically recounted the battles, he was a part of, did I realize the level of gratitude Coach Agase had to come home and play a game that he dearly loved and that was a huge part of his life.

    As he was finishing his story, which held our rapt attention, Coach AG advised us to be forever grateful for the opportunities we had that day, and those that lay ahead. He implored us to have gratitude for our families, teammates, friends, and school.

After hearing his story, he did not need to tell us to be grateful for the great country we lived in and the freedoms that we have and often take for granted. The emotion in his voice made that perfectly clear.

Coach Alex Agase was an All-American college player, NFL player, college coach, decorated United States Marine...and member of the "greatest generation."

An Attitude Of Gratitude

Dave Meredith (teammate), Coach Alex Agase, myself, and Doug James (teammate) at the Rose Bowl Stadium, in Pasadena, CA, the day before the 1983 Rose Bowl.

What I've learned

1. Oftentimes, we take for granted the good things we have in our lives.
2. Gratitude is the art of noticing and savoring what is good in your life.
3. Don't underestimate the positive effect that expressing gratitude can have on someone's life.

What you can learn

- Expressing gratitude helps you focus on the positive aspects of your life.
- Developing an "attitude of gratitude" is a choice you make and control.
- When a person is grateful, they look for the "good" in others and demonstrate gratefulness through encouragement.

Challenge question

What are three things you are grateful for?

Bible verse

Deuteronomy 24:11 – "Be grateful for the good things that He has given you and your family."

Postscript

I last saw Coach Alex Agase in late November 2006 at a memorial service for Coach Bo Schembechler, who passed away earlier that month. Even though his body was failing, his mind was still intact. With a strong voice and clear eyes, he stated to me and my two college roommates—the same roommates and former players who were with him on the sidelines of the Rose Bowl decades prior—that he was forever grateful to have coached players and men like us at the University of Michigan. I, too, am forever grateful to have the opportunity to be coached by a man like Alex Agase.

[4] https://www.usmcu.edu/Research/Marine-Corps-History-Division/Brief-Histories/Marines-in-World-War-II/Battle-for-Iwo-Jima/

[5] https://www.nationalww2museum.org/war/articles/okinawa-costs-victory-last-battle

CHAPTER 12
POWER OF THE POSSE

"You never fully appreciate what you have until you don't have it anymore."

-Glen Beck

Community: A unified body of individuals who share a common interest.

The negative effects of the global pandemic continue to manifest themselves daily as we move beyond that tragic period of our history. The government and self-imposed "lockdowns" during the pandemic seemed like the safest and most logical choice to limit the spread of the virus. However, in retrospect, the devastating negative effects of people being unable to meet, gather and socialize in a community atmosphere may never be fully measured.

One of our greatest human needs is to belong. We're not just social beings; we're pack animals. If you disagree with this or attach negative connotations to being characterized with animals, ponder for a moment about how people from all walks of life form cliques with others throughout their entire lives.

These social units, that we naturally form from the womb to the tomb, serve as our "community".

Humans are not meant to be alone. For a full life, rich with meaning, we need to surround ourselves with others. A community can give us a sense of belonging and identity, help us learn and even keep us healthier in body, mind and spirit.

The following statistics illustrate a few negative aspects humans face when the benefit of a "community" is not present in their everyday lives[7]:

- One in four Americans report that they have zero friends to confide in on important matters. This statistic has tripled in the last thirty years.
- One in three Americans over the age of 65 are socially isolated. One in two people over the age of 85 are socially isolated.
- Having weak social connections is as bad for our health as being an alcoholic and twice as bad as being obese.
- Social isolation sets off a cellular chain reaction that increases inflammation and inhibits the body's auto-immune response to disease. We not only go mentally insane from isolation and loneliness; we also get physically sick!

Think of it this way: Having friends is a natural stress reducer. Lower stress means a lower likelihood of stress-related illnesses, such as high blood pressure, heart troubles and gut issues.

As a member of a community, you have access to a support network of peers. Whether you turn to your community to commiserate, seek advice, or simply share your story, having a supportive group in your life can have a powerful effect on your overall well-being.

As I mentioned earlier in this book, there was a period of time in my life, following my graduation from college and the end of my athletic career, when I was met with the stark realization that the "community" I had belonged to and benefited from was no longer part of my life. Thankfully, this period was brief (less than two years), but during that time I certainly felt lost.

During my lifetime, I have come to value and appreciate the benefits of belonging to a community and the incredible blessings we have access to by becoming an active member of a community.

In a recent conversation with one of my esteemed clients and close friends, I was told that the group fitness sessions that I coordinate and lead at my training facility are the number one reason he continues to train with "us." The "us" he was referring to are the people that he trains with and has gotten to know who are part of his community.

I certainly will not take credit for the idea, creation or implementation of group fitness classes as the core of my business model as a fitness coach. The credit goes to God, who has given me gifts and talents and woven them together for the purpose of serving others and glorifying him.

Please allow me to give you a brief summary of how I got back into the fitness industry and was once again reminded of the importance and power that come from being part of a community.

It has been almost three decades since I relinquished control of my life to the Lord. During this time, I have learned that He speaks to His people through the Bible, fellow believers and circumstances. I have become painfully aware that it is prudent to be well informed of His teachings and follow His leads.

I chose to leave government service in 1996 and relocate back to the great state of Michigan, the place my wife and

I have always called "home", even during our decade away living in Arizona and Georgia.

After a brief, lackluster and costly stint as a sales rep/wholesale distributor, while contemplating yet another career change, I was led to attend a two-year course of study at a large Christian church in nearby Southfield, Michigan. Looking back, I can see how following this "leading" was a way for me to discover the gifts that I was given and how to use these gifts to glorify God and begin another career.

"Layperson's Bible School" was a two-year extensive study of the Holy Bible and was one of the most exciting, rewarding and enjoyable periods of my life. One of the main things I learned during the course was how God wastes nothing and that He uses all things for good for those who believe in Him. (Roman 8:28)

During a semester break from school, I took my son Jake to the grand opening of a retail fitness center near our home. He had expressed an interest in beginning a physical training regimen to become a better athlete. I knew the importance of this and was elated that he had made the decision to begin a training program that he continues to adhere to today.

While showing Jake around the facility, the owner/manager invited us to try out some of the "newest and greatest" Hammer Strength weight training equipment he had purchased for his facility. I chuckled and shared with him that I was very familiar with Hammer Strength, as I was tasked with designing and outfitting the Strength and Conditioning Facility at the Federal Law Enforcement Training Center during my previous career. I mentioned to him that not only was I familiar with the Hammer Strength equipment, but I was also a personal friend of the inventor of the equipment and had actually witnessed some of these machines being designed on a CADCAM computer before they went into production.

The owner observed me showing my son how to correctly use these pieces of exercise equipment and asked more questions concerning my background. He then asked if I would consider becoming a "Personal Trainer" at his facility. I chuckled and responded that I had never been a "Personal Trainer" and shared with him that I had recently left government service where one of my duties included the physical training of Federal Law Enforcement Agents. I further explained that I had never done one-on-one training but rather had trained groups of 24-48 federal agents in two-hour blocks of "hands-on" instruction.

He stated that personal training would be an easy task for me, and he needed someone immediately to train new clients that had already signed up for sessions at his facility.

I had to admit that I was intrigued and available. However, before I made another career decision, I felt it best to discuss this new opportunity with my wife prior to accepting his offer.

After a brief discussion with my wife, and agreeing to a more than fair compensation agreement with the facility owner, I began my third and current profession as a Strength and Conditioning Coach.

After almost two enjoyable and rewarding decades since I became a Strength and Conditioning Coach, I now own and operate a facility that specializes in group training sessions that are designed to enhance the fitness levels of people ranging in age from pre-teens into their seventies.

During this time, it has become quite evident to me, the trainers that work with me and my clients, that physical training on a regular, consistent basis in a group setting creates an environment where people can achieve higher levels of physical fitness while forging relational bonds within a community.

Group fitness has three key components that make it unique when compared with one-on-one personal training. The components are camaraderie, accountability and competition.

I have found that these components help establish a sense of "community" within each specific age group that allows a coach/trainer to attract new clients while maintaining and retaining current clients. In my opinion, the ability to attract, maintain and retain clients is the number one indicator of success, not only in the fitness industry, but also in other service-related businesses.

THE BENEFITS OF BELONGING TO A COMMUNITY

1. It's fun! Being together allows us to share circumstances in our lives that are funny and enjoyable. This helps to create happiness, reduce stress and is refreshing.
2. Creates empathy. You learn to relate to others who are facing struggles in their lives.
3. Sense of belonging. Becoming part of a community of like-minded people can create a feeling that a person is part of something productive and is proven to positively affect their overall attitude.
4. Decreases the feeling of loneliness. Feeling alone creates anxiety and depression. Connecting with others on a regular basis alleviates these feelings.
5. Provides a support network. It's good to have someone to confide in. Sharing life experiences and seeking advice from a fellow community member provides emotional support.
6. Helps with communication skills. Being an active member of a community requires communication and active listening skills.
7. Reduces factors that can lead to chronic disease. Isolation and choosing not to exercise is proven to lead to chronic health conditions such as heart disease, immune system issues and cancer.

Power Of The Posse

Athlete group training at the House of Iron during the summer of 2024.

Adult group training at the House of Iron during the winter of 2024.

What I've learned

1. Being in a community leads to personal growth.
2. You don't realize how important being a community member is until you are no longer part of a community.
3. Being a community member is a learning experience.

What you can learn

- Being in a community helps you see others points of view and allows us a chance to learn to accept differences of opinions.
- Being in a community gives a unified sense of purpose.
- Being in a community allows us the opportunity to become a better "net worker".

Challenge question

What benefits do you see from becoming a member of a community?

Bible verse

Hebrews 10:24-25 – "And let us consider how we may spur one another on toward love and good deeds, not giving up meeting together, as some are in the habit of doing, but encouraging one another—and all the more as you see the Day approaching."

Postscript

[7] Divine, Mark. (2024). Uncommon – Simple Principles For An Extraordinary Life. St. Martin's Press.

ABOUT THE AUTHOR

Lawrence "Jake" Sweeney is a 1984 graduate of the University of Michigan. He attended Michigan on a football scholarship and played in 48 consecutive games for the legendary coach, Bo Schembechler. Jake is a two-time Big Ten Champion and competed in four bowl games during his playing days.

After graduation, Jake pursued a federal law enforcement career and accepted an appointment to the 195th Session of the United States Border Patrol Academy. Upon graduation, he was stationed on the US/Mexican border in Douglas, Arizona.

In 1988, Jake accepted a position as a physical training instructor at the United States Border Patrol Academy in Glynco, Georgia. After serving in that capacity, he was offered and accepted a full-time position with the United States Department of Treasury as a Lead Instructor/Course Developer at the FLETC in Glynco, Georgia.

Shortly after his tenure with the Department of Treasury, Jake was offered and accepted a promotion as a Supervisory Immigration Officer with the United States Immigration Officer Academy, where he supervised and trained thousands of federal law enforcement officers in the following subject matters: strength and conditioning, non-lethal control techniques, defensive tactics and trauma management.

You're Allowed To Try

In July of 1996, after ten years of government service, Jake decided to pursue opportunities in the private sector and chose to relocate to his native state of Michigan.

As a parent of two young athletes who participated in hockey, volleyball and basketball, Jake was asked to help coach his children's youth sports teams as they traveled throughout Michigan and surrounding states. His passion for coaching and teaching was renewed, and eventually led him to establish "Jake's House of Iron" a "Performance Athletic Training Facility for Athletes and Adults" in Canton, Michigan. He has had the honor of helping several athletes pursue and achieve their athletic and academic goals of playing college and professional sports.

In 2023, Jake established MVP Performance Coaching to further assist, enhance, and develop the overall performance of people seeking to achieve their goals.

Jake continues to lead Group, Team and Private training sessions at the facility that bears his name in Canton, Michigan. He and his wife of 38 years, Dawn Otten-Sweeney, have three adult children, Jake, Auldon, and son-in-law, Cody, in addition to their first grandchild, Steele.

He and Dawn divide their time between Metro Detroit and Northeastern Michigan.

Book Jake Sweeney Today!

- In-Person Speaking Engagement
- Virtual and In-Person Performance Coaching
- Individual, Group, and Virtual Strength and Conditioning Training

For more information on the following, visit my website or scan the QR Code.

www.MVPPerformanceCoaching.com

www.ingramcontent.com/pod-product-compliance
Lightning Source LLC
Chambersburg PA
CBHW060532080526
44586CB00012B/704